This book is dedicated to

Lori Leedom

without whose love and support

it would never have been completed.

Contents

Introduction –

"Once social change begins, it cannot be reversed. You cannot uneducate the person who has learned to read. You cannot humiliate the person who feels pride. You cannot oppress the people who are not afraid anymore. We have seen the future, and the future is ours." ~ Cesar Chavez

There is something incredible happening in our world that some have already become aware of, others have started to sense, and which will eventually touch every single being on our planet. It is a change so profound that it will literally transform the world as you know it. It has begun and cannot be reversed.

What is this change? It is the next logical and most necessary step in our evolution. It is that which is required so *we can all begin to participate in changing our world* from what it is today—a place where a child dies every three seconds, thousands die every week from malnourishment, disease, neglect, and violence. Where there is so much suffering that every sixteen minutes, someone finds their life so unbearable that they decide to end it and commit suicide, to something vastly different.

This book has been written to help those who wish, sooner rather than later, to understand this change, begin participating in and benefiting from it now, and provide the tools which will assist them along the way.

One - How Our Consciousness is Changing, Who it's Happening to, and Why.

"Civilization is on the verge of a massive transformation in consciousness, one so profound that it will change life on this planet." ~ Bruce H. Lipton

There are very special moments—critical times in history—when a kind of quickening occurs. The last one occurred in the late 1800's just before the turn of the century. Until this period in time, our cutting-edge technology was represented by such crude items as the bow and arrow, telescope, and gunpowder. Then suddenly there came what is referred to as the Industrial Revolution, and in an extraordinarily brief period of time we discovered the internal combustion engine, electricity, television, radio, the telephone, the atomic bomb, and managed to put a man on the moon. How could this happen? What made it possible for us to advance more in a few years than we had throughout the entire rest of our existence?

If someone living in the late 1800's had been told of these impending technological advancements they would have found it difficult, if not impossible, to accept. Discussions of driving their buggy without a horse, flying through the air to different countries in mere hours, or men walking on the moon would have sounded like the ravings of a mad man. And yet somehow it happened, we went from covered wagons to convertible automobiles, from wind powered wooden ships to atomic powered submarines, from being earthbound to flying and actual travel into outer space. It's difficult to reflect on this enormous technological leap forward in such a short time and not wonder what made it all suddenly possible and why?

This book has been written to answer these questions and—more importantly—to tell you about ***another quickening which is occurring right now that will change our world forever.*** Our present time is another critical moment in history, and the urgent need for this intervention or quickening has resulted from the fact that our technology has outgrown our humanity. Without a corresponding increase in our consciousness to enable us to use our technology more wisely, our very existence is in jeopardy.

This quickening has nothing to do with mechanics, electronics, computers or any other technology. This time it's not something 'out there' in our world that will be changed, but rather each one of us, our very consciousness. Someone once said, "We only see the world darkly." This person was not the first, nor the last person to tell us that we do not see ourselves, or others clearly, and instruct us that the truth would set us free. It has been this inability to see each other and even ourselves that is at the root of all of our problems.

The current state of the world is not about our being inherently violent or evil creatures, but rather it is simply what has resulted from the low level of our present state of consciousness. To the degree that our awareness remains at this level, we will continue to create pain for ourselves and others. Another way of saying the same thing is "Unconscious of our unconsciousness, we make possible the unconscionable." This lack of consciousness is what is about to change. And as we finally become capable of seeing ourselves and others—not with our present distorted view—but clearly, as we actually are, hatred and anger will be replaced with compassion and love and our world will become a vastly different place.

Two - Seeing From a Higher Perspective.

"No problem can be solved from the same level of consciousness that created it." ~ Albert Einstein

This quote by Mr. Einstein tells us that we can never find a solution to any of our most serious problems (i.e. any of the many forms of violence, murder, etc.) while we remain at the same level of consciousness we were experiencing when we created them. This explains why, despite our best efforts (from our current level of consciousness), the terrible violence and suffering throughout the world continues. World peace will remain just a dream, wars will continue to be waged, and we will go on hurting and killing each other endlessly—as we have since the beginning of time—until what happens? Until we are able to see all of this from a different perspective, from a higher level of consciousness, which, because of the Quickening that is occurring, is becoming available to more and more people even now.

Anyone having read this far might be asking, "Well what's the difference between consciousness and higher consciousness?" or "What exactly do we mean by higher consciousness?" And that would be the perfect question at this point. Let's see if we can answer it right now.

Scientists and philosophers have been forever attempting to define consciousness with little real success. However, no deep philosophical discussions are needed here. We are going to keep it simple. For our purposes, we will define consciousness as being any state other than that when we are unconscious. In other words, when someone is not asleep, in a coma, or dead they are, by this definition, conscious.

The general theory is that our consciousness has moved up the scale as we have evolved. For instance, at one time it was thought that we had the simple consciousness found in animals. That is, we were aware of our environment but not conscious of ourselves, or self-conscious. This type of consciousness can easily be seen in cats and dogs with their complete lack of concern for their appearance. How much they weigh, how they are dressed, how their hair looks, or how old they are falls outside the scope of their radar. They simply are not aware of themselves in this way.

The next step up the evolutionary ladder is the level of consciousness we humans presently experience called self-consciousness. Unlike our pets, we are not only aware of our environment, but ourselves as well, that is, we are aware that we are aware. As a result, we do worry about how we look, how much we weigh, how we are dressed, how our hair looks, and so much more.

We imagine because we are aware of ourselves physically and seem to have some intermittent awareness of our actions that we actually are completely self-aware. This is where we need to take a second look and see if whomever came up with the expression 'self-aware' may have been perhaps a little too generous. Perhaps 'semi-self-aware' would have been a better choice, because in fact, it's much closer to the truth.

It is said that there are really three of us; there is the self we see, the self others see, and finally our real self. This simply but accurately illustrates the limitations of our present state of consciousness. We see ourselves—but not accurately, and we see others with this same lack of clarity. The most we can say is that we are, at best, only partially aware of ourselves. There is much we are unaware of because we have simply been incapable of seeing ourselves objectively. We act, but more often than we would care to admit, without knowing why. Do we decide to get angry, depressed, irritated, agitated, to like this person, dislike another, etc., etc., or does all of this just happen, while usually the 'why' goes unnoticed?

We can spend years miserable in a dysfunctional relationship without understanding how we got there, or how to escape. Then all too often when we do manage to free ourselves from one unhappy relationship we find ourselves quickly in another. The important thing to understand is that we go through all of our lives 'somewhat' aware of ourselves, but severely limited in our capacity to see ourselves or our world with anything approaching real clarity.

Considering that we get into relationships, take jobs, decide who we like and don't like, get married, and vote without the capacity to see clearly, how could our lives individually or collectively be any different than they are? The critical question becomes then, how do we begin to obtain the clarity needed to become truly self-aware and finally become capable of seeing ourselves as we really are?

Being truly self-aware would mean that we were capable of seeing, not the distorted and very subjective view we have of ourselves at present, but instead the truth. We would understand precisely our every motivation. In this state, we would see ourselves exactly as we are and no interpretation would be necessary. No one truly self-aware would ever need to read a book to try to understand themselves better or visit a psychologist in an attempt to interpret their actions more clearly. There would be no confusion such as "Why did I marry him or her?" or regret "I can't believe I did that?" Higher consciousness *is* true self-awareness. It represents freedom from all of the pain and suffering we cause ourselves and others...simply by being unaware.

This higher state of consciousness may sound very mystical and inaccessible, but we all experience the precursor to it as infants. In fact, this is our original state. We start out life as an observer. At that point, we are simply observing and experiencing what is. We have yet to form judgments regarding which of the things we see are 'good' or 'bad', 'better' or 'worse.' We simply see what is. There is no resistance to anything that appears before us, no deep-seated subjective opinions, no bias, no prejudice, no racism, no nationalism, not even the slightest preference, just pure observation and experience. I refer to this state as **The Original Observer.**

Later in life we have moments, mostly unnoticed, when nothing is happening, when we perceive, and for a brief moment the brain is quiet and once again we just see, we are once again the Original Observer. Then in a flash, we are back to judging, critiquing, desiring, rejecting, etc. and experiencing the (often painful or at least uncomfortable) parade of emotions which accompany this 'thinking.' These moments appear and disappear, normally without our even being aware that they occurred. This happens partly because during this time, there is literally nothing happening within us emotionally to make them stand out. We may not notice it, but during these moments, we are free of the incessant clatter of our mind and the resultant emotional reactions.

What the vast majority of beings who live and die on this planet never realize—never even suspect—is that this Original Observer is our vehicle to higher levels of consciousness. Mystics have known this since the beginning of time. It is not only the escalator to increased levels of consciousness, but the essence of every 'path' to enlightenment (which is really just a higher level of consciousness), regardless of who did it (Jesus Christ, Buddha, Krishna, Mohammed, etc.), where they lived, or what time in history it occurred.

In the next chapter, we will take a closer look at a typical example of how this incomplete awareness creates suffering for individuals, couples and entire families without anyone ever realizing what is actually happening. Don't be surprised if your awareness suddenly changes and you begin to understand the formerly unrealized motivations behind your past (or even present) behavior.

Three - The Effects of Being Only Partially Conscious.

"Our civilization is still in a middle stage, scarcely beast, in that it is no longer guided by instinct, scarcely human in that it is not yet wholly guided by reason" ~ Theodore Dreiser, *Sister Carrie*

Next, we are going to take a look at how a couples childhood conditioning and lack of awareness drew them together...and then tore them apart. We will have a unique opportunity to see this relationship from the inside. That is, through both her, and then his eyes, respectively. These individuals will share their most intimate feelings and tell us what they believe caused their marriage to fail. Then, finally, we will take a look from the standpoint of higher consciousness. What you see from this higher vantage point may well change your view of yourself and your relationships forever.

A view of a life from normal consciousness

We will start with Kathy. She is attractive, intelligent and, if asked, will say she is successful and happy. Her friends would describe her as loving and kind. Her ex-husband would strongly disagree with both of these last statements. She is in her mid 50's and has a daughter and son from her first and only marriage.

Short history and an actual interview with Kathy

She describes her mother as timid, especially around her overbearing father who she says was always emotionally unavailable and, at times, physically abusive. From a very early age, Kathy witnessed her mother's fear of her father. She not only saw—but was often subjected to—his violent outbursts. Watching her mother cower in the face of her father's aggression angered Kathy. She loved her mother but could not help feeling disgusted when she saw her become weak and helpless, something she swore she would never be.

She began responding to her father's intense anger with her own, stubbornly refusing to ever back down. Her older sister, rather than her mother, was the one who would comfort her after these encounters. The tension between Kathy and her father continued to escalate. The angrier he became, the angrier she became until the inevitable occurred, he began to strike her. As Kathy entered her teen years, the confrontations with her father grew in both frequency and intensity, until at the early age of 15 she left home.

Question: Kathy, can you tell us what it was about Robert that caused you to fall in love and then marry him?

Answer: Sure. He is handsome and in the beginning was very charming and sort of swept me off my feet. He had a great sense of humor and was quite romantic. I felt like he really loved me, but I made the mistake of thinking he would remain that sweet, thoughtful guy forever.

Question: So Kathy, what happened?

Answer: Shortly after we were married things began to change. He started to change, we stopped laughing and he quit courting me. Over time, he became increasingly distant and started getting angry a lot. We began fighting about almost everything. I came to see who he really was; a self-centered, heartless man who didn't care about me or his children.

Question: What finally brought you to the point where you were ready to end it?

Answer: It was after a number of really big blowouts. I had left him a couple of times...at least for a while, but then I would have a weak moment and go back. Then suddenly, one day he informed me that he was in love with another woman and leaving us.

Question: There must have been times when you felt very alone.

Answer: Yes, I did. My sister moved away at one point, but thank goodness for my daughter. I don't know if I could have gotten through all of that without her.

Kathy's view of things

Kathy believes that she tried very hard to make the relationship work. In her view, Robert was a con man who just pretended to love her to get her to marry him. That, in truth, he was a cold, heartless person completely incapable of loving her. She said their arguments became very intense and she had become very afraid that he might hurt her.

Kathy has never been able to figure out why she has had such poor luck finding the right guy. She rarely meets a man who interests her, and when she really falls for one, he always turns out to be emotionally abusive. She hopes one day to meet Mr. Right and at last find true love. She says she is generally happy with her life, but finds herself increasingly lonely and that the thought of spending the rest of her life alone both frightens and depresses her.

She has enjoyed the closeness that she has shared with her daughter, but feels more and more as if that relationship is slipping away. She is not close at all with her son whom she describes as dishonest and says he is frequently verbally abusive to her. At one point, she had to tell her son it was time for him to get out. He did. She says he has many personality traits similar to his father that make it difficult for her to be around him for more than a few moments at a time.

Another view of her life from a higher level of consciousness

Now let's take a look at what is really happening in Kathy's life. Let's see what Kathy is unable to see for herself. You could share all of the information that follows with her, but it just wouldn't register, she would be absolutely sure your assessment was wrong. ***She is simply not capable of seeing her life objectively as a result of her present level of consciousness.***

Kathy would like to have someone to share her life with but, as we said, is simply incapable of being aware enough of her own behavior to understand what the real problems are or how to fix them. She does not see that the cause of her problems is not 'out there,' but rather 'within her.' She doesn't see that because she spent so much of her life resenting her father that it literally became a habit and when this habit manifested itself after she got married, she unconsciously transferred those feelings to her husband. Then, as a result, she became increasingly distant in the relationship (exactly the way her father did with her) which caused her husband to feel unloved, lonely and eventually seek comfort in another relationship. When he did this, of course, it confirmed Kathy's picture of him as 'bad.' She is unable to see that the behavior her husband was unconsciously driven to is a reaction to her own negative behavior, that she is, in effect, the architect of her own unhappiness.

Neither can she see her powerful need to become the wounded child and again be comforted as she was by her sister. Or how this compulsion forced her to demand nurturing from her young daughter at a time when she should have been instead giving it. Even now, her codependent daughter struggles to give her new husband the primary place in her life he deserves, but which her mother still occupies.

She does not see that her reaction to her father's anger and coldness, that is, becoming angry and cold herself caused her to be much more like him than she would ever be willing to admit. And that this learned behavior, now turned on her son, has driven them apart. Or how this alienation of her son deprived him of the most important relationship with a female he will ever have. She cannot see that she predisposed him to similar problems in every future romantic relationship he will have. The core problem is that at her present level of consciousness she is not capable of seeing her negative conditioning. The result? It is impossible for her to have a meaningful and lasting relationship with any man.

Kathy certainly didn't choose her negative conditioning, so how did it happen? When she was a child, she felt certain emotions repeatedly, before, during and after the encounters with her father. The negative emotions included anger, resentment, loneliness, and rejection, which consumed her for hours upon end. After these bouts with her father (when her older sister came to her rescue while playing the role of surrogate mother), she received the closest thing to love she would ever experience in her childhood. To her, when her sister sided with her and shared her resentment for their father, it felt like love. Keep in mind that these moments where she received 'love' could only occur after the confrontations with her father, she became conditioned to feel that the negative feelings were part of the subsequent feelings of love. And this became a pattern that she would unconsciously recreate over and over, (as she did with her husband) without ever realizing that she was doing it.

Why does she keep creating situations where she feels those emotions again? Because when the body experiences emotions over and over, we become addicted to them. Emotions we feel are literally created by chemicals produced in our body and we can become hooked on them exactly as we can on cocaine or any other drug.

During her childhood, Kathy became addicted to these two groups of emotions she experienced, fighting with her father and then being comforted by her sister. Once this addiction was well established, her future was set. After that, no matter how much Kathy said she really wanted to be happy; her body/mind addiction would recreate her childhood melodrama over and over again endlessly.

When Kathy left to get married, she took her clothes, jewelry, and also her emotional addictions along with her. Psychologically she wanted to be happy, but was totally unaware that her body wanted—needed like a junky needs their drugs—to feel those emotions from her childhood again and again. To satisfy her addiction, Kathy (unconsciously of course) had to set the stage so she could recreate her childhood melodrama. Her husband was given the role of her father (the bad man) and initially her older sister played her original nurturing role. When her sister was no longer available, she turned her daughter into a surrogate sister (the show must go on), partially robbing her daughter of her childhood.

Was Kathy ever, even for a moment, aware that she was unconsciously recreating the melodrama of her youth? No. And it is unlikely, at her level of consciousness that she ever will. Instead, her understanding will always be quite limited, and she will never be able to experience real happiness. I know what you are thinking...are there any of these unhappy scripts running in your life?

The answer is that everyone has their share, until they are able to become conscious of them and do a little psychological pruning. They are like weeds in a garden that must be controlled if the garden is going to grow and become healthy and beautiful. The real problem is, like Kathy and Robert, at your present state of consciousness you will be unable to see clearly, what they are. You may be able to see the effect, that is, a broken marriage, strained relationships, inability to reach your potential or some compensating behavior like drug use, porn or alcohol, but not the actual cause. The good news is that with the increase in your capacity to see yourself which is resulting from this Quickening, coupled with the information in this book and a little work, you can begin to see and begin to be become free of, all of these types of patterns in your own life.

A view of another life from normal consciousness

This time our subject is Robert, Kathy's first husband. He is a successful sales manager for a cellular phone company. He is nice looking, intelligent and, if asked, will also say he is and happy. His friends describe him as outgoing and friendly. He is in his mid 50's, married just once and his only children are those he had with Kathy.

Short history and an actual interview with Robert

Robert says his family was pretty normal. But he does remember his mother and father arguing intensely from time to time. He says his father was a good man, but that they were never really close. His father traveled quite a bit and spent most of his time on the road. Robert's mother had a difficult time adjusting to her husband's chronic absence and was often in a bad mood. Robert says she would start feeling unhappy and then it would almost always lead to her getting really upset and taking it out on him, sometimes physically. He says he really did love his mother when she was not, as he put it, pounding on him. Robert left home at 18.

Question: Robert, can you tell us what it was about Kathy that caused you to fall in love and then marry her?

Answer: What I remember most about Kathy when we were first together is that I enjoyed being with her, though she was rather moody. However, I seemed to be able to cheer her up, most of the time. I enjoyed seeing her happy and would often do something silly or surprise her with some small gift. Then we would have a great time together. It made me feel good to be able to make her happy.

Question: So what happened?

Answer: Well everything was fine for a while. We got married and I was very happy, but it became increasingly difficult to bring her out of those dark moods. It started feeling like she was constantly unhappy, only now it was me she was unhappy with and I couldn't seem to do anything to change her mood no matter how hard I tried. It was almost like the more I tried the worse things became between us.

Question: What finally brought you to the point where you were ready to end it?

Answer: As time passed and I found myself helpless to bring Kathy out of those negative states and I started getting more and more frustrated. I really loved her, but the constant rejection started making me feel depressed all the time. She treated our daughter more like a girlfriend than a daughter and turned her against me. Then, instead of just Kathy being upset, I would have to deal with this constant anger and resentment from both of them. It was unbearable.

I was pretty sure she just didn't love me anymore, nearly everything I did upset her. It seemed pretty clear that it was just a matter of time before she left me or got involved with another man, if she wasn't already. So—and I know I shouldn't have—I started seeing a coworker. She is actually similar to the way Kathy was when we first met before she became constantly upset. Anyway, I just felt drawn to her and one thing led to another.

Robert's view of things

Robert believes his relationship with Kathy when they were first together was great and then, for some unknown reason, she turned on him. He feels that he did everything possible to make the relationship work and suspects that Kathy just fell out of love with him, and that she would soon leave him. He knows that cheating on his wife was wrong, but feels he was powerless to do anything about it under the circumstances. He strongly resents Kathy for turning their daughter against him, but insists that he was never rough with her physically and could never have hurt either of them.

He says he has an easy time meeting women, but a very difficult time having a happy, long-lasting relationship with one. He believes that women are way too emotional, often unstable and cannot be relied upon. He has started to wonder if he will ever find the enduring, peaceful relationship, he says he craves.

Another view of his life from a higher level of consciousness

Now it's time to take a look at what was really happening with Robert. Let's see what Robert is unable to see. As with Kathy, you could share all of the information that follows with him, but it just wouldn't register. He's simply not capable of seeing his life objectively as a result of his present level of consciousness.

We can see that Robert, like most people, would like to have someone to share his life with but has the same problem as his former wife; he is simply incapable of being aware enough of his own behavior to understand what the real problems are or how to fix them. Neither does he see that the cause of his problems isn't 'out there,' but rather 'within himself.'

He doesn't see that during his formative years, he spent much of his time trying to somehow keep his mother from becoming unhappy so he wouldn't have to deal with the anger and rejection which inevitably followed. Or that the reason he fell in love with Kathy in the first place was because their relationship gave him an opportunity to feel all of the emotions (created by chemicals in his body) he had become addicted to as a youth.

He never understood that Kathy's addiction to unhappiness and anger was what drew him to her in the first place. She allowed him to experience all of the emotions his body was addicted to. He had no way of knowing that, like any addict, both he and Kathy would need more and more of their particular drug (the emotions they felt chemically in their bodies) to get the same feeling. This is the reason for the escalation in the frequency and intensity of their disagreements. At his present level of awareness, all of this was simply beyond his comprehension. He never suspected that he too was the creator of his own unhappiness.

Until he is able to see himself from a higher perspective, that is a higher level of consciousness he will never find the lasting happiness he desires. He will constantly find other women whose childhood conditioning will result in their needing to be cheered up, women who will always move toward greater unhappiness and make him feel the same rejection he felt as a child.

All of the problems Robert and Kathy had were a direct result of their inability to see themselves or each other clearly. This strange form of blindness is responsible for the vast majority of suffering in the world. That may sound like an exaggeration, but we have just seen how it affects individuals and couples alike.

Proof of this statement can be found by asking the following questions: If we could really see the pain we cause ourselves and others, is there any way we could continue doing it? Please take a moment and think about that question seriously. If we could really see the horror and uselessness of war, could we continue having them? And finally, if we could see all of the suffering that is occurring in the world is there any way we could keep from doing something to stop it? It becomes crystal clear if one considers these questions earnestly what the problem actually is...we are powerless to change these things because we simply don't see them clearly.

The next chapter will be for many, the beginning of the end of their blindness. They will begin to see that which has been hidden from them previously, and they will begin to experience freedom from this useless suffering.

Four - Understanding the Difference Between 'How We Are' and 'Who We Are.'

"The main obstacle to man's development is his lack of knowledge about the nature of consciousness itself."
~ David R. Hawkins, M.D., Ph.D.

We know that Kathy started out as the Original Observer, simply experiencing what is, with no emotional highs or lows. If you created a graph to illustrate her psychological state at this time it would look not unlike a straight line, neither rising (being happy) nor dropping (being unhappy) very far, just consistently joyfully aware. We all start out in this blissfully impartial state and then something happens, we begin to get conditioned by our life experiences. We begin accumulating *pairs of personalities* that I refer to as **disparate extremes**, which—all together—will become our composite self, literally, who we come to believe we are. Understanding these disparate extremes in yourself and others is essential to your becoming more self-aware and beginning to live your life more consciously.

The brain, in its attempt to store information that is vital to our survival, has a mechanism to help this storage occur at times, very quickly. This mechanism is emotion. Our brain reasons that if there is a certain level of emotion related to an event, it must be important. The intense emotion tells the brain that it needs to record this information and keep it available for future reference. The experience of strong emotions is how these pairs of personalities are formed in us. The more intensely an emotion is felt, the stronger it is imprinted on our neural brain circuitry until eventually it becomes permanent. If the stimulus is great enough, this imprinting can result from a single incident.

The way we learn is by our neurons creating connections during our initial exposure to anything new. This then influences the likelihood of these same neurons firing together in the future, that is, our remembering whatever it was that happened. This is referred to as "Hebb's Hypothesis" and is named after the psychologist physician, Donald Hebb. He summarized this process by stating that *"Neurons which fire together, wire together."* Our capacity to remember anything is based on this process.

And it is how we individually make connections with an experience and determines how we will react when we encounter it again. Pavlov training a dog to salivate at the sound of a bell is perfect illustration of this.

Take the example of a child with the misfortune of having been brought into the world by parents who will abuse him. One moment, he is the Original Observer, just watching and experiencing what is. Then suddenly something overwhelmingly traumatic happens. He finds himself being attacked by the very people he believed would protect him, his own mother and/or father. This child, of course, responds with feelings of extreme fear and helplessness. Because of the intensity of the event, these feelings are deeply etched in the nervous system in this child's brain. These emotions have now been stored for immediate recall *exactly as they occurred.*

When he encounters another fearful situation later, instead of reacting with a degree of fear appropriate to that specific situation, this child experiences *the exact same intensity of fear he felt originally.* His brain has now been wired to react to fear in the extreme. If on a scale from 1 to 10, with 1 being ever so slightly fearful and 10 being unbearably fearful, his original fear was felt as level 8, that is how he will tend to experience every extremely fearful situation for the rest of his life. He will consistently feel too much fear. He is now limited to this single response regardless of whatever fearful situation might occur. And it is important to understand that when this reaction occurs, it is not that he is remembering those feelings, but rather that *he will actually re-experiencing them, that is, he will feel exactly the same degree of fear and helplessness as he did when they occurred originally.* This same conditioning can occur with anxiety, sadness, depression, or any other emotion.

In the case of the abused child, we saw how a generalized fear response was created in him by this experience. By 'generalized' I mean that, instead of responding in a specific way to whatever event occurs in his life (being aware, seeing what is happening in the present and responding consciously) he is limited to this one general, very intense, response to any fearful situation.

Along with this fear and helplessness, the child experienced intense rage, which he was unable to express, rage, which was his brains response to the intense fear and feeling of helplessness, the sort of thing that happens to a corned animal. When it realizes escape is impossible it turns and attacks ferociously. So, in addition to a generalized fear response, he also developed a generalized anger response and will respond with this same intensity of anger in certain situations even though it may be completely inappropriate. It has now become his generalized response when he becomes angry.

You can see that once this conditioning takes place, the child no longer has anything to say about how he will respond in a fearful situation. ***This initial traumatic childhood experience has already decided for him.*** In a completely reflexive way, that is, without his considering what is happening presently, he will always tend to react to a fearful situation by replaying those emotions *with the same intensity* he did originally. His response to a fearful situation in life will happen in the same way that one's leg jerks when the doctor taps their knee with his little hammer. Stimulus and immediate response, without any conscious mental activity occurring, it just happens.

This explains why battered children usually become battering adults. When they become angry, they become too angry, and that same rage they felt as a child will now be turned on their offspring and the cycle of abuse will continue. We see the same generalized response in people all the time when something relatively minor happens but they respond with what is obviously far too much fear, anger or some other emotion. Perhaps you have even experienced this yourself.

All of our emotional responses get 'set' during these early years of our life. Another example would be someone who is continually told they are stupid. They will internalize that belief and find it very hard later in life to feel otherwise about themselves. They may overreact if someone corrects or even disagrees with them. Perhaps another person grew up with lots of brothers and sisters with whom they fought constantly, had to share everything with and were never given much privacy. As an adult they may find themselves uncomfortable living with anyone, even their own wife or husband. The list of examples is endless and we all experience some form of this conditioning as children.

What sorts of conditioning did you experience that now undermines your relationship with your significant other? Do you find yourself at times unhappy, angry, or dissatisfied without really know why or what to do about it? Doesn't everyone? And did any of us really have anything to say about the conditioning we would receive—that is, how we would come to react to life? Have you been able to see what makes you unhappy and free yourself from it completely, once and for all? Until The Quickening, and without the tools for change that are now becoming available, no one has. It is extremely important to understand that, in the same way you have been unable to change some of your conditioned responses to life, *so it is for others*. Please read that last sentence again, it is absolutely essential to understand that we are the product of our conditioning.

And when you see someone whom you believe is acting badly, understand now that they have been trapped in this behavior that was conditioned into them without their consent, and that this behavior causes them great suffering as well. What is needed is more compassion, first for ourselves when we see how we are at times compelled to do things which result in our suffering, and then for others as we see they too suffer in the same way.

This information is being made available because we are becoming ever more capable of truly understanding it. And this new understanding will begin to change your level of awareness. You may be coming to see that people with the conditioning we have been discussing never respond with intense fear or anger by choice. If that is true, then who, you may ask, is in the driver's seat when these automatic reactions occur? Who decides? The answer is their conditioning.

You will know your consciousness is changing if the next time you see someone respond to a situation with what seems like excessive anger, your understanding of the situation is different. What you never saw before will begin to become apparent. Now, you may be capable of understanding that this person is not making a conscious decision to be angry, it is just happening, as a result of their faulty conditioning. It is simple, reflexive, unconscious behavior.

Your new level of awareness will result in a much deeper understanding of this person and allow you to avoid responding with your own conditioning of anger or resentment. For instance, you will know that their response is a result of intense emotional and possibly physical pain they experienced in their youth, and you will feel compassion. You will know that their parents or whoever traumatized them probably did it repeatedly throughout their childhood, and again you will feel compassion. You will be able to see that they are a victim of their own behavior and that the quality of their life (their job, their relationships, and even their health) is significantly reduced by it, and you will feel even more compassion. You can measure the change in your consciousness by your ability to react to 'difficult' people, less and less from your own conditioning and more and more from a place of compassion.

Experiencing this type of seeing (from a higher level of consciousness) will change you. It will help you move from your normal conditioned response to someone's behavior to a more conscious one of pure compassion. You will no longer see them as a 'bad' person, but rather as just another human being who experienced suffering as a child, and, through no fault of their own, became conditioned to behave in a way that creates suffering for themselves and others. It may even allow you to have compassion for yourself when you unconsciously react to what is happening in your life in a way you later regret.

Normally, when we get upset, we don't question it at all. It happens so quickly that we don't really have time to think, because it is that reflexive behavior we were conditioned with as a child. We believe it's our own personal response, when nothing could be further from the truth. The reality is that this behavior was not part of your original equipment—you weren't born with it. It is actually something quite foreign, something alien that was added without your asking for or consenting to it.

When someone sees clearly that their personality is, for the most part, not really theirs at all, but simply something created in them in response to the people and events they were exposed to as a child, they will no longer feel the need to remain identified with it or defend its every action. They will no longer be held captive by this behavior and be condemned to believe "That's just who I am," a belief which keeps them a prisoner of their conditioning and powerfully eliminates any belief—and therefore any possibility—of change.

They will know better. Instead, they might say, I can see now that this is some conditioning I received due to the circumstances of my youth and it may or may not be something I wish to keep. **I will decide.** It could be seen as conditioning that resulted in behavior that they wish to alter or eliminate entirely. Now, because they no longer take ownership of it, they can be more objective, more conscious, in their manner of dealing with it. They will no longer have to be imprisoned by, and suffer from it for the rest of their life.

Imagine a situation where you were about to enter a car race and someone came up to you and said, "Those tires will never make it, you would be much better off switching to these specific tires." or "If you want to really compete in this race I would change your four barrel carburetor to an eight." Probably you would thank them for their insight and do what they suggested. Most of us are able to accept this type of impersonal (it is not about us) advice with no problem.

Unfortunately, when it comes to receiving constructive criticism about ourselves, the situation is quite different. If in the previous example the owner of the car was strongly identified with it, they would react quite differently. Instead of accepting information, which would be of great help, and being appreciative, they would probably become angry and say something more like "My tires are just fine! What makes you think your tires are any better? And who are you to tell me my tires are bad?" This would result in their refusing any help and no doubt having a problem later on.

This same identification happens when anyone tries to tell us anything about how we might change our personality for the better. Because we see this personality as who we are, any criticism of it is taken too personally, as if they are saying we are somehow defective. It makes us feel bad and we become defensive. This identification with who we have become programmed to be represents an enormous barrier to any personal development. As long as we hold on to this idea that **how we are is who we really are,** any chance for change will be remote. Only by separating ourselves from this notion, can we really begin to see ourselves objectively and finally begin to find our way back to our true self.

Once we fully understand the distinction between 'how we are,' that is, our present conditioned responses to life, and 'who we are,' the real person we would have become without the dysfunctional conditioning, we are finally free to begin the search for our real selves and let go of behavior that is inconsistent with our true nature. Perhaps you are actually a very loving person, but as a result of your conditioning, act in ways that are very different from this. It may be that you have been conditioned to believe that you must overachieve in life and have become a workaholic, when in reality you would be much happier working less and spending more time with your family.

Or it may be that you have been programmed to believe you are defective in some way and so live a life far below your true potential. People in general see any suggestion for change as an indictment, an expression that they are in some way flawed. This is where a huge paradigm shift is needed. Every single one of us has grown up in a dysfunctional world and internalized some of that behavior—everyone—with no exceptions. We need a complete reversal of our present view. Instead of seeing the need for change as something negative, it should simply be seen as something everyone of us wants to be involved in and is willing to help others with to bring ourselves more peace and happiness in our lives.

What could possibly be more unproductive than desperately holding on to behavior, which causes us to continue suffering and keeps us from attaining real happiness or reaching our actual potential in life? We need to see that we can only become truly happy by letting go of the false idea of who we have always thought we were and actually finding out who we really are underneath the dysfunctional conditioning. When we clearly see the difference between 'how we are' and 'who we really are' and the world of possibilities that creates, the idea of change becomes very exciting.

When we investigated the relationship between Robert and Kathy, we saw that they were unaware of the conditioning that was undermining any chance for happiness they might ever have. Kathy couldn't see that she was projecting all of her childhood feelings for her dad onto her husband or that, entirely without her knowing it, she was actually addicted to all of the negative emotions her behavior was creating. She says she wants to be happy, but the question is; will happy ever be an option for her as long as she is unable to see herself objectively? Sadly the answer is no.

And Robert says he wants to be happy, but unconsciously selected a mate that would guarantee he felt the unhappy emotions of his childhood over and over. He left Kathy for another woman with the same issues, and who will wind up feeding his chemical additions and he will suffer again. He says he wants to be happy, but because of his limited consciousness will never experience it, at least not for long.

As your consciousness increases, you will see that Robert and Kathy's situation was not so much an exception, as the rule. You will see more and more how much suffering people experience— and cause—simply because they are not truly conscious of themselves. You will begin to feel more and more compassion for everyone around you that suffers in this way.

These automatic conditioned responses are not limited to anger and fear. As your consciousness expands, you will see connections that previously went unnoticed. Whenever you see someone suffering from anxiety, depression, or any other unhappy state, you will know that this present behavior is the result of some traumatic or chronic event in their past. You will understand that their body felt those emotions over and over and they eventually became addicted to them.

It will be clear to you that they are, without actually being conscious of it, recreating in the present, circumstances that will allow them to feel these unhappy emotions, and suffer again. You will feel great compassion for these individuals as you come to realize that they are creating—unknowingly—their own useless suffering and that there is nothing anyone—including you—can do about it until they experience a change in their level of consciousness.

We have seen how the people we have been discussing thus far, with nothing to say about it, become conditioned to feel too much anger, too much fear, etc. They become incapable of reacting to the present moment objectively; instead, their conditioning is running the show. What's important to understand is that we all—without our consent—get conditioned by life in a similar way. No one ever asked the battering parent when they were a child if it would be ok to batter them. They were never asked if they would mind becoming the kind of person they feared and hated as a child. Yet, without their permission, this is exactly what happened to them.

Each of us gets left out of the decision making process during our conditioning, we are unwilling victims of whatever dysfunction occurs in our lives. Then later, we actually become unconscious accomplices in this crime by failing to see this behavior as something quite alien when we take ownership of it. We never asked for it, we didn't have any say so regarding what conditioning we would or wouldn't care to accept. For better or worse, we just get stuck with it. We may not have had a choice then, but the real question is...do we have a choice now? Do we have to continue being what other people have made us, even if it brings us chronic unhappiness and pain?

Did Kathy or Robert have a choice? Do most of the people you know seem to have the capacity to choose happiness in their life? How can anyone choose to be happy when they are unable to see the true cause of your unhappiness? The vast majority of people are so identified with their conditioning and so completely unaware of the actual forces that run their lives that change is impossible. They neither see the true source of their problems nor have the tools to change themselves. So it is quite easy to see the first rule of change: *You can only become free of your conditioning (the unseen forces that create unhappiness in your life) to the extent that you are willing and able to see (be aware of) it.*

So it's easy to see why so few people have been able to solve the recurring problems in their life, they have not yet been able to see that they are not their conditioning and then begin to work against it using the type of tools available in this book which all fall under the heading of what we refer to as Dynamic Neuroplastic Mediation® or DNM for short.

Five - The Possibility for Personal Change is Far Greater Now Than Ever Before.

"The greatest revolution of our generation is the discovery that human beings, by changing the inner attitudes of their minds, can change the outer aspects of their lives." ~ Rumi

In the last chapter we discussed how, as we are growing up, the emotional events of our life shape our thinking and, in fact, determine how we feel about almost everything. Had we grown up wealthy instead of poor (or vice versa) our political view might be quite different. Had we not been so strongly disciplined, we might manage others more effectively. If we had not had a parent or parents who were emotionally unavailable we might feel more deserving of love. We could continue to be ruled by our dysfunctional conditioning for the rest of our lives and cause suffering for ourselves and others countless times in the future...or, the time may have come when the capacity and the tools for change like DNM are finally available, at least for those who have the good fortune to hear of them. You may ask, why wouldn't everyone know of these incredible techniques for change?

A Quickening occurs not so much like the domino effect where one domino strikes another and then another sequentially. It is more like a cascade where one domino hits two which then hits four, which hits eight, etc. This process happens quickly, and does not involve just a few isolated people, but continues spreading to everyone until it finally reaches the general public. These Quickenings happen rapidly, but not instantaneously. There is always a bit of a lag which occurs between the discovery itself, the verification that it is real, the general acceptance by the scientific community, and then especially before it's passed on to us lay people.

For instance, at this very moment, numerous areas of research are unearthing discoveries that will forever change the way we perceive ourselves, and the world in which we live. But, as before, because there are so many and they are all so new, most have yet to reach the average person.

How many people, for example, have ever heard of Neuroplasticity, Transcranial Magnetic (or Electric) Stimulation, Neuro-Biologic Reset, Dynamic Neuroplastic Mediation, Psychoneuroimmunology, Conscious Neuroplastic Mediation, Eye Movement Desensitization and Reprocessing (EMDR), or Conscious Neuroplastic Integration? And yet these are some of the most powerful techniques for personal change ever discovered.

Take Neuroplasticity for example, it is the discovery that **you** can—with mere thoughts—change, not only the function, but *the actual structure* of your own brain! Imagine, you can actually change the physical structure of this critical part of your anatomy—which determines who you are—*just by thinking*.

Find this hard to believe? Well, you're not alone. In fact, you are in pretty good company. Santiago Ramon y Cajal, the renowned Spanish neuroanatomist and winner of the Nobel Prize in Physiology and Medicine didn't believe it either. In a treatise on the nervous system, he published in 1913, he said, "In the adult the nerve paths are something fixed, ended and immutable." His view of the brain with its circuitry hardwired and unchangeable might as well have been chiseled in stone. For almost a century, all of the leading neurologists accepted, without question, Cajal's opinion as the absolute truth.

During this time, all of the 'experts' told us that the brain, unlike all other parts of our body, was given to us with a certain number of neurons (nerve cells), that neither their structure nor number could ever be changed. As recently as 2004, Neuroscientist Fred Gage summed up the prevailing view as follows: "If the brain was changeable, then we would change. And if the brain made wrong changes, then we would change incorrectly. It was easier to believe there were no changes. That way, the individual would remain pretty much fixed."

This fatalistic, but widely accepted view has had a profoundly negative effect on any notion we have had regarding our ability to change. Because it was considered the truth by neurologists, it was automatically accepted by the vast majority of physicians, psychiatrists, psychologists, and other mental health care professionals. All of whom, without realizing it, spread this misinformation to their patients (the general public), and as a result, we have all simply taken it for granted that we cannot change our own brains.

Would it be possible to measure the negative impact this generally accepted notion regarding our inability to change has had on the generations of people since Cajal's declaration? Is there anything that could be more limiting to anyone's personal development than convincing them—before they even start—that any real change is impossible?

Fortunately, for us this 'fixed' idea of the brain has been completely refuted. And while it is true that you are who you are because of the unique pattern of neural connections in your brain, we now know that these neurons are in a constant state of flux. The notion that 'you are who you are, and there is not much you can do about it' has finally been laid to rest.

So, these neural connections that determine our very identity are not hard wired and can be changed. But just how do we go about doing that? Well, the expression 'use it or lose it' sums up the situation very well. If you think the same thoughts every day and have the same feelings and reaction to life constantly, you are reinforcing those neural connections and they will become stronger and stronger.

So, each time we are inattentive and simply allow our conditioned personality to run unmonitored without any attempt to control it, we increase its power over us. That's the bad news. The good news is, using DNM and the collection of tools it provides, some of which you will be given in this book, along with your now greater capacity for self-awareness, you will be able to take control. And as you decide to think different thoughts and have different feelings and reactions to life, the old connections will begin to weaken and over time disconnect entirely. You can shape your behavior and become the person you want to be rather than remain trapped in whatever conditioning happened to you as a child.

Let's look at a practical example of putting this ability to change to work? Let's say you saw some aspect of your behavior that you wish to alter. What would you do? The first and most important step would be to move up (with the help of the DNM tools you will soon be given) to a different level of consciousness which will allow you to stop 'being' the conditioning (feeling angry, irritated, or whatever), and instead 'see' the conditioning (see that there was anger, irritation, or whatever). This different perspective is essential for any sort of change to occur.

To continue our example, let's assume that the behavior you wanted to change was the frequent irritation you feel toward your significant other whenever you find yourself having to wait for her.

Scenario One: It's Saturday night. You have both decided you want to go out for a romantic dinner. You are ready; however, she is still having trouble deciding what to wear. At this point, you have 'become' the irritation. No system within your body remains untouched; your body is producing specific chemicals related to your state of mind. Your heart is beating faster, your blood pressure has increased, your skin is slightly flushed and a stream of negative thoughts have begun to flow through your mind. It won't be long before some caustic remarks are made. She is hurt by what you say, begins to withdraw from you emotionally, and the course of the entire evening is changed, and not for the better.

Scenario Two: It's Saturday night. You have both decided you want to go out for a romantic dinner. And you are ready; however, she is still having trouble deciding what to wear. At this point, utilizing the DNM techniques you will be given, you will have the capacity to decide not to 'be' your conditioning and become irritated, you instead 'see' this conditioning wanting to run you. The systems in your body are affected, but less than they would be otherwise. Instead of being lost in a stream of negative thoughts, you watch—but don't go with—what you see. Something very different has occurred. YOU ARE SEEING, NOT BEING THE CONDITIONING.

Soon enough she is ready, and because you were patient with her, she responds by becoming more affectionate and you both have a delightful evening. And most importantly, your ability to 'see' rather than 'be' the conditioning weakened it. The next time it will be even easier to resist, then even easier the next, until eventually it will cease to exist.

What we saw in Scenario Two is but one example of how DNM gives us the power to begin changing our conditioning to significantly increase the quality of our relationships, or even keep them from ending. With these tools, we can eliminate depression, anxiety, fear or any other negative emotion that is causing us to suffer uselessly, and do it without the use of semi-successful prescription drugs many with serious side effects. We can even utilize these new skills to eliminate behaviors that may be keeping us from achieving real success in life.

So we know that change is possible, now the big question is how can one consistently 'see' rather than 'be' the conditioning as they always have. Answering that question is the focus of our next chapter.

34

Six - The Pitfalls Along the Path to Change.

"Your thinking is like a camel driver, and you are the camel: it drives you in every direction under its bitter control." ~ Rumi

In the last chapter we saw how the very thoughts we allow ourselves to have from moment to moment actually shapes our brain. As a result of the Quickening, we are beginning to have the power to pay more conscious attention to our thoughts—to literally change, not only the way we think, but the very structure of our brain. It means we can free ourselves from self-destructive habits and create ever more happiness in our life beginning right now! However, if we ignore the increase in consciousness that is trying to occur within us now and pay no attention to the thoughts that come into our head, as is normally the case, then something quite different can result. We can wind up with a literal cesspool of negativity.

Ok, so now we know we don't have to remain the person someone else conditioned us to be. Thanks to the Quickening and tools that are becoming available like DNM, we are finally beginning to have the power to recreate ourselves. Now, with this new capacity to see, WE CAN DECIDE. We see that, if we really want, WE can be the architects of our personality. Now it is normally at this point in some self-help book where you are told something like "Ok, you beautiful person. I have bestowed on you all of my great wisdom and now you know, not only that you need to change, but why, how it will help you, and what specifically you need to change so...go, go and do it!" Sound familiar?

But always the question of exactly how to make that change gets ignored. Some suggest that you make these life-altering changes by simply being in the moment, or thinking positive thoughts. Of course, if you could do that, you wouldn't be reading their book. Or we are told things like, "Make a really firm decision for change today!" like you haven't already tried that. And of course, there are the other suggestions like "Just be love," or "Open your heart," or "Learn to accept what is." If it was really that easy, you would have already done it, right?

This same situation occurs when we go to church, synagogue, temple, or whatever. We are told to love they neighbor, be truthful, not to think about sex, etc., but again, they leave out the HOW. So in the end, it turns out we don't love all of our neighbors, in fact, it's quite possible that we really can't stand some of them. We try to be truthful, but to be honest...we are not always. Fortunately the 'not thinking about sex' part is easy so we actually can do that. Ok, so much for being honest.

We would love to change and be more honest, to really love more selflessly, and be happier. We would like to stop getting irritated, angry, anxious, or depressed. But the truth is...**we have never been given the tools we need to do it.** And to make the situation worse, everyone acts as if change were actually possible for themselves and others, in the face of overwhelming evidence to the contrary. Are people changing and letting go of their anger? Is violence decreasing? Are couples changing and learning to be more loving? Is the divorce rate going down? Are more and more people learning to let go of their fears, anxiety, and depression? Are fewer people taking antidepressants, anti-anxiety medicine, or self-medicating with drugs and alcohol?

Of course, we all know the answer to those questions. It is really important to understand that we have all been brought up in a society that demands tremendous change, when so little has been possible. In the end, we simply become hypocrites, repressing our true feelings as best we can—pretending to be changed—and paying a terrible price both mentally and physically.

Finally, because of The Quickening and the powerful techniques for change that are being discovered like DNM, real change is possible! We can stop trying to change and actually mold ourselves into the person we want to become. We can really become more loving, more compassionate, free ourselves from debilitating negative emotions and significantly increase the quality of our lives.

At this point I could begin sharing with you DNM's powerful techniques for change you will find later in this book, techniques you are no doubt anxious to learn. However, if I did that I would be jumping the gun, so to speak, and doing you no favor. It would be a little like showing someone how to play a video game without also telling them about the obstacles they would encounter immediately and how to avoid them so they could continue playing. Unless you know what to expect once you begin using these techniques, your ability to 'win' the game against your conditioning will end very quickly.

So, just as someone giving you directions for getting through the forest might tell you about the lions and tigers and bears (oh my!) that lie in wait, I will offer you a warning of the booby traps and pitfalls along the path to change.

The first barrier we will discuss has to do with **the way your memory develops.** During the first couple of years of our lives we develop what is called implicit memory, later comes the explicit memory and is what we use for recalling facts and personal events. The implicit memory is also called the procedural memory because it helps us remember processes or procedures, like how to tie our shoes or ride a bike. It is also the repository of our preferences and is where the feelings of like, dislike, etc. are stored. These feelings are mostly unconscious to us. We may like this color or that flavor, but be unable to explain why.

When we are first viewing the world, we have no frame of reference, no stored data to relate to. We just take it in, accept it, without any ability to first edit or evaluate it. At this point, we are like a clean slate and whatever experiences we have plant themselves in our psyche without the slightest censorship. This is not the ideal situation; these early experiences stay with us our entire life and often influence how we feel more than anything we experience throughout the rest of it. An example of this might be a young girl who, during this period of time when her implicit memory was her only tool, is told she is unattractive. She will continue to feel this way for the rest of her life, even if she grows up to be a very pretty woman. Intellectually she may know that she is considered attractive, but emotionally she will continue to feel as if she is not. Our implicit memory pre-determines how we will react in a given situation and it is completely automatic.

We all know people who suffer from this inability to change their view of themselves or the world regardless of what new information they receive. There are those who believe they are unintelligent when the truth is just the opposite, but their belief that they will fail keeps them from even trying. Then there is the person who believes that every woman will desert him and so acts in a way to create that unnecessary reality for himself. You may be able to think of examples related to your own thinking that you know intellectually are incorrect, but that still influence you just the same.

If we are unable to alter these unconscious beliefs that seem indelibly written on our mind, how can we ever change? This has been the big problem with traditional talk therapy. Someone might have an irrational fear of flying (or whatever) that is related to information stored in their implicit memory and no amount of dialogue will ever change their view.

Simply talking to someone and explaining that their thinking is incorrect and needs to change is completely useless and can never help. So what does? Still not wanting to jump the gun, I won't say anything other than there is something that does work, something that will allow you to change ineffective programming stored in your implicit memory. For now, what is essential is that you know about this tendency in yourself, and when the moment of truth arrives, be able to see it for what it really is.

The next barrier to personal change is an extremely powerful foe; it is **our very own body.** What? How could that be? I will explain. The first thing to understand is the connection between our thoughts and our body. Every time we think something, our brain and body instantly releases chemicals which race through our body. The biochemical reactions which occur as these chemicals arrive at, and are received by, various receptor sites in our cells results in our being able to *feel* what we think. There is a chemical recipe produced for every possible emotion.

What happens next is very interesting. Your body responds to a thought by having a feeling, and then the brain responds to the way the body is now feeling by producing thoughts consistent with those feelings. So we wind up caught in a loop where there is a thought which causes a feeling which causes more thoughts which cause more feelings, and on and on. This is the way we get 'stuck' in a negative state. We think something, which makes us angry, we then feel angry so the brain produces more angry chemicals, which make us even angrier, and there we are, trapped in this unhappy place.

To make the situation even worse, the more frequently we experience anger, the better our body gets at feeling angry. Our cells develop more receptor cites for anger and our brain produces larger quantities of the chemical of anger.

Addiction is the feeling that results from a chemical rush that is experienced as it cascades through the body by way of an assortment of glands, ductless glands and the spinal fluid. When someone is addicted to a drug, say heroine, it is because taking heroine causes the brain to produce chemicals, which are then experienced by the body in the same way it experiences any other feeling. And this potential for addiction that the body has is not restricted to just positive or pleasurable emotions. *The body will become addicted to any chemical state it experiences repeatedly.* So it can be seen how one could become addicted to an emotion they experience repeatedly in the same way they become addicted to drugs.

The idea that we could become addicted to sex (the feelings the body associates with sex) is not so hard to grasp, but it probably sounds strange that we can become addicted to unhappy feelings like anger, fear, sadness, or depression, and yet it is true. Take the example of someone who constantly and consistently in their youth had a parent or parents who scolded them intensely and told them they were worthless. During these verbal assaults, their body would react by producing specific chemical states, i.e. feelings of shame, sadness, and anger. Over time, their body would have gotten use to these feelings and actually become addicted to them. It would need to feel those feelings again in the same way a drug addict needs their drug. This helps us understand why people who say they are miserable with their partners continue to stay in those relationships for years, sometimes their entire life.

Look around you at the number of people you know who continue to smoke, drink, do drugs, over eat, stay in unhappy marriages, remain in jobs they hate, or in other difficult circumstances when no one is forcing them to do it. You might now see that they may not be getting what they want, but they are definitely getting what they (their body) needs (and has become addicted to). Yes, there is a way out of that trap as well, but again, it is very important that you are able to see this tendency in yourself when the time comes to deal with it.

The next barrier to change is **the mistaken idea that we can change by just reading (this book for instance) or listening to someone talk.** If that were true, why with all of the "get rich quick" books and CD's out there, are so many people still living from paycheck to paycheck? Why, with all the diet programs, exercise equipment, and supplements are so many people still overweight? Why, with more information available than ever before on self-improvement, are so few people changing their lives? And why, with all of the material available for couples to improve their relationships, is the divorce rate continuing to rise?

The reason all of this reading and listening has not (and will never) help us change those aspects of our lives, is because receiving information—by itself—is inadequate. New information plus the same old behavior (same type of thinking) equals zero. *Receiving new information cannot change us.*

We must first develop the ability to become more conscious, which is coming to us now during this Quickening. Then it's finding a way to actually put this new information into practice in our lives. If we could figure out how to do that, *then,* we could achieve something. But, as long as we continue to store up more and more data, without developing new skills (changing how we do things); we can expect nothing but the same results. We could read until we go blind, attend church every day of the week, and listen to CD's endlessly, but it will all come to nothing because—in the end—we will still be the same. We may know more, but *we will still be the same*, that is, have the same thoughts and reactions to life as before.

We make the mistake of thinking our lives will change, as if through osmosis, by simply reading, or hearing someone else speak. In truth, *the only way we can ever change, our only hope, is to change our thinking by learning to 'see' instead of 'be' our thoughts!* Our thoughts literally create our lives, and as long as we have the same types of thoughts, *we will continue to create* the same experiences in our life.

You could read a book on boxing, and afterwards be able to discuss bobbing, weaving, jabbing, and the importance of footwork, etc., but your ability to defend your self would not have improved. Only a certain period of very specific and intense exercise would enable you to actually put into practice what you had read.

This practice would consist primarily of changing how *your body* reacts in certain situations. Specifically the way it responds to various types of attacks. The level of your new skill would be directly related to the ability of your body *to react in a new and improved way*. These new reactions would then allow you to achieve different (better) results.

After this training you would be changed, your body would respond differently than before. You would not be the same, and your chances of defending yourself would be much greater. *The outcome would be different because you had changed and acquired a new skill, not just more information.* No longer would it be something you merely knew, it would be something *you could do*. You would now have an ability that you would never have developed by simply reading about boxing.

In the same way, if you want to change some behavior i.e. how you eat, approach business, or relate to your significant other, you (your thoughts) must become different; your mind must respond in a new (and improved) way, not stay the same as before. You cannot continue to think in the same way and get different results.

What has been missing in everyone's attempt to change their lives is the ability to remain conscious of their thinking (see rather than be their conditioning) and a similar type of practice as that mentioned above, a very specific and intense exercise for *the mind* that is required *to change how it reacts*. DNM will provide these techniques, but you still must practice them, not just read about them. Only then can the information received, do to our greater awareness become useful. Just as reading about boxing, by itself, did not result in your being able to defend yourself, so reading about how to have a better relationship with another person, your work, your money, or your body is simply not enough.

Someone who is reading about weight loss is a perfect example. They probably know more about food than most non-dieters, but are unable, *because of certain kinds of thinking*, to put this information to use. Until they have *identified* and then *changed the thinking* that causes them to be unhappy and compels them to overeat, all of the calorie counting and diet aids (information) in the world are useless. As long as the cause, *how they think*, remains, so will the effects of that thinking, their overeating.

The same is true of someone trying to become successful in business, happy in a relationship, or change any other aspect of his or her life. More information simply won't help. They must learn to approach these situations in a new way. They cannot keep going down the same road and expect to wind up in a different place! You cannot remain the same and expect your life to change.

Just like the previous example of our weight conscious person, someone who is angry and withdrawn is never going to have a happy relationship with someone else *until they change,* that is, think differently. Someone who is fearful is never going to become a successful entrepreneur until they learn by controlling their thoughts to rid themselves of excessive fear, and learn to think about money and business differently. You simply cannot remain the same and get different results from life. That is impossible. Yet it is precisely what everyone is trying to do and the reason why success is so rare.

So, if we are going to change in any way, we must first see our situation from a higher level of consciousness, which will begin to allow us to control the way we think. We have to realize that we are, at present, ruled by our thoughts, and that *the quality of our lives is determined entirely by the type of thoughts we experience*.

If we are happy, it is not because of what we happen to have or even who we are with, it is a direct result of *how we think*. The extent to which we are successful in life, the types of relationships we have, even our health to a large extent is all a result of the type of thoughts we have. This is why any possibility for change must begin there.

For anyone who does not believe their thoughts control them, or see how they are subjected to this endless stream of dialogue that determines how they are going to feel at any moment, there is a simple exercise you can do to verify this for yourself; while looking at the second hand on your watch, try to stop all of your thoughts so that not a single word comes to mind, not even the thought "I will not think" for three minutes, just complete silence. If you are in a quiet place where you won't be bothered you might try it now.

After you attempt this, if you are honest with yourself, you will see that it cannot be done. Within seconds, the mind, though you are trying to stop it, goes on rambling like a disobedient child. We are subject to this "disobedience" from the time we wake up until we finally escape it in sleep. We are forced to listen to thoughts that result in our feeling angry, fearful, sad, or depressed, as well as other negative emotions that dramatically affect our actions and, we are forced to listen whether we want to hear and be affected or not.

The above exercise shows how little control we have to stop the incessant flow of thoughts that constantly assail us. Until we have learned to change our mind, this often hurtful and unproductive dialogue will continue to hold us back from our true potential for success and happiness.

Instead of our thoughts being consistently productive and helping us to achieve our goals, they are in constant conflict. Some of our thoughts help us, and some hold us back. Until we learn to control our thinking; we will always be pulled in different directions as our thinking changes. We are at the mercy of whatever thought comes to mind.

It is sort of like being on a ship headed in one direction, then suddenly there is mutiny and some of the crew wants to go to a different location, then another part of the crew takes control and heads back the way they started. Or we could use the example of someone deciding not to do a certain thing, and then a short time later deciding (as a result of having different thoughts on the subject than before) they really should do it. If we could control our thinking, we could always be headed in the same direction and success would be easy.

Most people never notice it, but this endless stream of thoughts we have, comes all by itself, *completely uninvited*. At any moment, we can be taken away mentally without ever choosing to do so. We might hear an old song on the radio, smell a familiar fragrance, then instantly we are reminded of some experience in our past, then off we go on a mental sentimental journey.

The important thing to realize is that we do not decide to think the thoughts that follow the song or the smell. *It is as though we get left out of the decision making process*. There is the stimulus, the automatic thought response, and then we have to experience whatever emotion results. No freedom to choose our response or chance for a fresh, more objective evaluation of the situation, just our usual conditioned response.

We go to someone's house for the first time, and when we get there, something about their house reminds us of another house we saw that brings back pleasant or unpleasant memories and we begin to re-experience that instead of seeing *this* house and being truly aware of it. Or, we meet someone for the first time and they remind us of someone else we used to know and we are similarly affected. In both cases, our experience is diluted. We are forced to try to experience something new, while we are re-experiencing something that happened in the past. In the end, our new experience was watered down to the point where we can barely remember what happened. Proof of this is easily obtained by trying to remember how often you forget the name of the person you were just introduced to? You didn't remember because most of your attention was dealing with your thoughts rather than perceptions.

Sometimes (actually most of the time) this happens without our being aware of it and we find that we are "for some reason" drawn to or repelled by a person we just met. Our experience of this person is influenced by our past and *we don't really see them as they are,* and cannot until we are free from this associative thinking.

The net effect of all of this is that we go through much of our day not seeing things as they actually are, but instead we have everything we experience edited by this type of thinking. We lose our objectivity. It is as if we are not really there once this type of thinking has been triggered; instead, we are off remembering something from the past, imagining what might happen in the future, or altering the present in some way through our constant associations with past experience. We are simply not in the moment able to experience objectively what is happening.

When I first started paying attention to this phenomenon in myself and actually seeing the extent to which it occurred, I felt like a television set getting channel surfed by someone with a very short attention span. First one group of thoughts would come, then another stimulus, followed by yet another group of thoughts. All without my conscious involvement! I was simply a spectator, and this is what happens to all of us. We are the television without any say about what is shown on us.

46

It is possible for you to learn to control your thinking (rather than the other way around) so that all of the thoughts you have are consistent with your goals. That is, so you are not, at times, subject to other, very different thoughts, which pull you in the opposite direction. Learning to control your thoughts by employing the techniques of DNM allows you to regain control of the channel changer and decide for yourself what type of programming you will experience. If we don't want a sad show to play (on us), we can change it. Instead of a fight scene (occurring in our mind with someone at work, our significant other, or someone else) we can choose something more peaceful.

Imagine yourself able to have a conversation with someone about to jump from a bridge, someone who had 'decided' life was no longer worth living and was about to throw away this incredible gift. If you could look past their superficial explanation of why they were there and see the truth, you would see that they had been brought to this point, not because of a lost job or loved one, not because their life was unbearable or because of whatever sad situation they were in—but because they could not control the constant flow of intensely negative thoughts running through their mind. They are ready to do anything to be free of the pain those thoughts bring, even if it means ending their life.

Are there other people who have had a similar, or even worse, experience than our precariously perched friend, but who have not chosen to take the big dive? Of course, the difference between those individuals and this soon to be departed fellow is *the type of thoughts they have* in response to what has happened to them— not the circumstances of their life—*just the way they think*.

Going to the other extreme, if you were to spend time talking with someone who was very happy with their life and peaceful, you would see they had predominantly happy and peaceful thoughts. You could undoubtedly find other people with more money, better living conditions, etc. than this blissful individual, but who do not enjoy this same peace and happiness. Again, the difference would be *the types of thoughts they have.* Same circumstances, just different thinking resulting in a vastly different life experience.

Take the example of a man in a relationship who suffers from certain insecurities, that is, *(uncontrollable) thoughts* of themselves as unattractive, not worth loving, and unable to keep their mate interested to the exclusion of all others.

These thoughts will in turn cause them to have other thoughts such as "She is not really going to a meeting tonight; she is going to meet *him*." Or "She is only going to the meeting tonight because *he* is there" (this is but one example of the type of thoughts this person would have in various situations).

An endless number of similar examples, that is, other negative thoughts he experiences could be given. If he could control the negative thoughts he has about himself, he would not be having these suspicious (negative) thoughts about his mate.

It is not difficult to see where this chain of thoughts (or one similar) will lead. The other person comes home from a hard day at the office, more tired than usual because they had to go to a meeting they really did not want to attend (they had no secret motive for going, they simply went because their job required them to be there) and what do they encounter? Someone who is loving and compassionate? Someone who is going to make the rest of their night better? Hardly.

When they arrive they will have to deal with someone who is cold, distant, or even angry; someone who will treat them as though they were guilty of betrayal. Their exhausted state coupled with the others person's negativity will most likely result in an argument, and could easily spell the end of the relationship, if not this time, then the next, or the next. The insecure person's fear that they will lose the others love can literally cause it to occur.

This person's insecurities will cause them to be at times jealous, moody, angry, and in general not very enjoyable to be with as a result of those thoughts until the other person in the relationship is literally driven away. *These negative thoughts will bring about exactly what the person feared most!* And what is important to understand is that this situation only occurred because he created it (with his thinking), it didn't just happen. Then, of course, he will have even more negative thoughts after the loss occurs.

In his next relationship he will become even more desperate for someone he can trust, more insecure because of what he imagined (thought) happened in the last relationship, more afraid that it will happen again, and as a result, the next relationship will have even less chance of succeeding (because he will have an even greater tendency toward negative thinking). The cycle will continue endlessly until perhaps he finds himself looking for a bridge from which to jump.

When we are not able to remain sufficiently conscious, our thinking is like a wild horse that simply runs away with us most of the time. How do we pull in the reigns and finally get control? As we have seen, trying not to have negative thoughts doesn't work, nor does trying to have positive thoughts. What's the answer? In the next chapter, you will discover that...it's not what you think.

Seven - An Introduction to Dynamic Neuroplastic Mediation.

"You must be the change you wish to see in the world"
~ Mahatma Gandhi

Some people will be more interested in personal development, that is, how to free themselves from the conditioning that keeps them from achieving anything near their true potential in life. For others it might be a desire to end a long period of depression or anxiety. And no doubt, there will be many who are looking for ways to create a more deeply loving relationship, or to keep one from ending.

Whoever you are, and whatever problems you may be experiencing in your life, the starting place will always be the same...to become more conscious, that is, to be able **to 'see,' rather than 'be,' your conditioning.** Until this capacity for seeing begins to develop, no lasting change can ever be attained. So how exactly does one achieve this?

The most recent research has revealed new information about the workings of both the left and right hemispheres of our brain. Simply put, it was formerly thought that the left side of the brain was detail oriented, practical, handled words and language as well as math and science, and dealt with order and pattern perception. And that the right side of the brain used feelings, was 'big picture' oriented, employed imagination, responsible for spatial perception, presents us with new possibilities, and was involved in risk taking. However, thanks to these latest developments in technology we now have a larger view of the actual functioning of these two hemispheres.

Studies have shown that when we are in the process of learning anything new, the right side of our brain becomes quite active. Then, once something becomes learned and this new data is stored away and has now becomes familiar, we shift to using the left side of our brain. *The implications of this knowledge are enormous for understanding the difference between being more or less conscious.* We can see that when we are first learning something we actually are more aware—more conscious—and then, once this learning phase is complete we quickly shift to a less conscious, more routine response to that activity.

A perfect example is what happens when you first learned to drive a car. You were very aware of the feel of the door handle, the weight of the door, the way the steering wheel felt in your hands, your senses seemed to be (and were in fact) heightened during the entire experience. You were more conscious. You were acutely aware of every aspect of that event. This is what happens whenever we are learning something new, when we are really paying attention; when we are using the right side of our brain.

Of course, after you have been driving for a while, you can get in your car, drive somewhere and afterwards have only a vague memory of the entire experience. That is because the entire process has moved to your left-brain, it is now part of your programming, and you no longer have to think about or pay much attention to it. You do it, *but with far less awareness.*

This type of programming where we simply reference our prior knowledge without having to pay anything but minimal attention is essential and designed to help us perform all of the complicated tasks necessary from the moment we wake until we retire at night.

Imagine if you have to pay attention to where you placed your foot getting out of bed, adjust your balance, and think about where the other leg should move so the other foot was placed properly so you could walk. Needless to say, it would slow you down considerably. So this process of making everything we do automatic is a great help to us in life and enables us to perform countless activities with little or no attention.

What's important to understand here is that we not only create automatic patterns for walking, driving a car, or any other physical activity...*we do precisely the same with mental activities.* Our view of ourselves, our parents, and the world in general becomes data stored away for automatic retrieval. And in the same way we can drive our car with little or no attention, simply responding to data previously stored in our brain, so do we begin interacting with others in this same stimulus/response manner.

Once we have a frame of reference regarding almost anything, away we no longer see it with the same clarity we had initially, we simply respond from our conditioning. Our interactions have much more to do with our programmed response to a person or their pattern of behavior than they do with the reality of what is actually happening in that moment.

This activity of the brain where everything we experience is quickly converted into some automatic pattern and stored in the left hemisphere is, as I said, extremely useful. Unfortunately, it also results in our simply reacting to life automatically from our conditioning rather than actually being more present and capable of choosing other options. We have conversations with others, make decisions, consider the situations that occur in our life, and so much more all in this automatic way.

If our programming includes the idea that we are inadequate in some way, even if this is not the truth, we will continue to act (more correctly, react from our conditioning) as if it is. All of our feelings about what is 'right' or 'wrong,' when it is appropriate to get irritated or angry, even our political and religious views all begin to simply become our conditioned response, based on experiences far in our past, rather than an objective response to what is happening now.

The more we allow this to happen, the less aware we are in the present and the more incapable we become of adapting and growing. So what can we do to activate that right side of our brain to allow us to increase our consciousness and begin responding to life from a place of greater conscious?

As I mentioned in the first chapter, we all start life as, what I call the Original Observer (OO), this is you viewing the world with a sense of wonder, seeing what really is and being in a state of constant learning—it's all right brain activity. Everything is new and you are consistently in a place of heightened awareness. Colors are more vivid, smells more intense, sounds and textures are richer. Then as we build up our repository of knowledge of the world, that is, more and more data gets stored in the left side of our brains, we actually see less and less and instead recall more and more. Instead of seeing what is, we begin to simply associate our experiences with what we already know. Our perceptions are no longer happening in real time, but rather being recalled from an earlier experience in our life. Instead of reacting to the reality of the moment, we are simply responding to a generalized memory. Real seeing gets replaced with associative remembering. The more we accumulate routines and habits, the less active our right brain becomes. We gradually move from truly experiencing what is, to instead experiencing our generalized memory of it. So, the answer to becoming more conscious is to begin to re-experience your OO.

Now, I'm going to tell you something you already know...but have forgotten. Something that will slowly begin to come back to you as you continue reading. At first, it will feel a little odd, perhaps even a bit strange. But then, it will start to feel slightly familiar, and eventually over time, it will begin to feel more real to you than anything else.

Your OO is still there, it never left. It's there, seeing what is, exactly as it is. However, because it's nothing other than pure awareness, it doesn't captivate your attention like your ever changing and much more intense thoughts and emotions. It has always been there, like the stars are always there, it has just been buried beneath the constant static going on in your head. Beneath all of the 'shoulds' and 'shouldn'ts,' beneath all of the judgment, fear, anger, and desire for whatever you want in the moment. It's still there; we just have to get in touch with it again.

And it's not so much that you have to develop some new capacity, as it is about rediscovering what you already know, but have simply forgotten...but not entirely. There have been moments of stillness when you are not thinking anything, or at least not paying much attention to the chatter in your head. Moments when you felt a profound sense of calm until the next group of thoughts and emotions came along like a rowdy gang and took 'you' with them.

Your conditioning took over and has been in charge for a long time. It likes that role and enjoys being the boss. It is not going to easily give up control to your OO (Isn't it interesting how the double O's look like two eyes, without any expression, just watching?).

The difficulty with beginning to once again notice and maintain awareness of your OO is quite similar to what happens with your sense of smell. As you go through your day, you notice all of the smells you encounter, like the smell of your food, your coffee, and even the way others smell. You are perfectly capable of detecting these odors, but the smell of your very own cologne that is on *your* body and there every day escapes your awareness completely.

So how do we reacquaint ourselves with something so familiar that it's seemingly invisible? It's easiest to recognize your OO by what it's not rather than what it is. It is not a thought...it's not an emotion; rather it's the absence of either of these.

It is simple, pure awareness. It's what we begin to experience when we let go and relax. When...for a moment...our thoughts continue...but they seem very far away. In moments like this...we are no longer driven by whatever thoughts happens to find their way into our head...they seem incapable of touching us...we've temporarily grown ever so bored with all of that incessant dialogue...and it simply passes by barely noticed.

Some people are perhaps starting to sense it now. Can you feel yourself letting go of thinking...of feeling? What subtle shift in your awareness do you notice? Do you find yourself becoming still...quiet, and simply seeing what's there around you...including your own body?

Normally our attention and all of this energy that flows with it is going in one direction, away from us. But when you begin to experience your awareness of what's out there...and simultaneously...you find you are also aware of yourself, this will be the beginning of your re-experiencing yourself as your OO. It is a feeling of splitting your awareness between what you see and yourself simultaneously.

What begins to happen is that, instead of all of the energy flowing out and away from you, half of it will now be flowing back toward yourself. *As you are reading these words, you could begin to feel it by allowing half of that energy (your attention) to turn back to yourself and experiencing what that feels like.* The feeling is very subtle at first, but if you do it, you will feel yourself relaxing and your consciousness expanding. The more you practice this, the more powerful the experience.

It is important to distinguish this type of awareness from simple self-consciousness, which is always just your conditioning concerned about how you look, what others think of you etc. In those moments, your attention will be focused primarily on yourself and feels quite different from the experience of your OO.

When you are truly experiencing yourself, again as the OO there is a sense of letting go of yourself (your conditioning). It will be a feeling of simply being aware, without being anything in particular. It will feel as if your awareness is expanding beyond yourself, but, as I said, it is ever so subtle and requires you to simply sense its presence. Your mind may try to get involved and analyze or theorize, however, that type of activity will only impede your progress. **Your OO is above your mind and your mind will never lead you to it.** Nothing you think will do anything but get in the way. But you can, if you will let yourself relax and *just feel,* begin to sense it again, just slightly at first, and then more and more profoundly.

Please stop and take time to really make this something you are not just reading about...but are able to actually experience. Stay with it until you can actually begin to feel it, however slight. Only then should you continue reading. Nothing else in the book will be of any use to you until you actually begin to feel your OO again, and then only to the extent you are willing to commit yourself to work every day, as often as you can remember to deepen that awareness.

Because your OO is more aware, it's also more objective and intelligent. When you're trying to figure out what to do in a particular situation, your mind will normally respond from your left-brain conditioning. This severely limits your options. It is possible that your usual automatic response may be the best one in that situation, but it's just as possible that the opposite could be true. In any case, going with this sort of automatic 'thinking' always limits us to a very narrow range of possibilities.

Here is an example of how conditioned thinking works. Let's assume that you are in a relationship with someone and sometimes it's good, and sometimes it's really not. So you decide to 'think' about what you should do. Almost certainly someone in this situation would find themselves considering but two possible options; to end the relationship (during a period when they were feeling upset), or 'decide' they should stay and work it out (during a period when things were going well). Normally, this swinging from "I should end it" to "I should keep trying," repeats itself over and over.

If things get bad enough the relationship may, and often does, end. Because the person involved was limited to only the possibilities their conditioning offered they were unable to see any other options. Worse yet, they will find themselves in a similar relationship again soon enough and the entire process would simply repeat itself. When someone is not capable of seeing their conditioning, they are condemned to continue to be in it, and as a result, be draw again and again into the same life situations.

Einstein's quote *"No problem can be resolved from the same level of consciousness that created it."* is worth repeating here. **As long as we try to solve problems that our conditioning has caused us *while still in our conditioning*, we can never get far.**

Let's take a look at the above example of being in the relationship we just discussed and how, if we were freed (even partially) of our conditioned response, we would begin to be able to see more clearly what was really happening.

If we had been practicing being our OO during this relationship, we might begin to see patterns emerge. Our perceptions would be less emotional and so not confined to our usual conditioned response. We would develop a larger view which would result from our not being so intensely focused on this relationship and the problems we were having in it. We would be more capable of stepping back, so to speak, and more objectively comparing this relationship with others we have had. And because of this higher, less attached view we could possibly see something, which we had not been aware of before.

Perhaps we would notice that our current relationship is not so different from our last one. In fact, we may begin to be aware that this pattern of selecting a certain type of partner seems to happen over and over again. Where before, we would have been unable to see why we were compelled to repeat this pattern, we would now know it was our conditioning at work.

Knowing most of our conditioning originated in our youth, and looking from our OO, it is possible that we could now become more able to make a connection between our adult and childhood relationships. We might see that we seem to be seeking partners who will enable us to experience the same emotions we felt as a child. For example, we might see that we have been unconsciously selecting partners who will make us feel unaccepted and who are emotionally unavailable in the same way one or both of our parents did.

Seeing that we have this conditioning, which drew us to this person who would invariably make us unhappy, or angry, or whatever it might be, enables us to finally begin changing this pattern. Suddenly we have other options. And knowing that we always play an active role in recreating the melodramas of our youth, we might even begin to see more clearly our part in actually stimulating our partner toward certain behavior.

At this point, we would be able to approach this relationship from a more conscious place rather than from our usual conditioned response. We could see that we could change the dynamics (*our* behavior) and possibly improve the relationship. And most importantly, we would see what changes we needed to make—not from our conditioning but—from our OO. And because of this, our efforts would be moving us toward a more functional (happy) relationship with our self and our mate, instead of just repeating the same dysfunctional behavior as before. We could share what we have come to see with our significant other, allowing them the opportunity to join us in this process.

If our mate refused any attempt at change, or even if they did, but we saw that, in this particular relationship, we keep falling back into the same old patterns, we might decide that the relationship is unsalvageable. And that we need to use our newfound knowledge to find another partner with whom we could actually be happy, rather than seek out someone else with a complimentary neurosis with whom we could once again experience the same unhappiness.

This, of course, would necessitate our being aware of our conditioning that would tend to draw us to the wrong type of person again, the conditioning that would tend to push the next person we are with to become the wrong type of person, etc., etc. All of this would give us a chance to begin having a different quality of relationship. Only this view from a higher state of consciousness would enable this transition to occur, which could eventually allow us to have a truly conscious and happy relationship with someone in the future.

As you observe and listen to your friends and their problems, you might begin to see that they too are trying to solve the problems their conditioning creates—*from their conditioning,* which is why they remain continually stuck. They are simply unable to see what's really going on or what they might do to change. This is why relationships so often end and the divorce rate continues to soar.

The same situation occurs with employers/employees, coworkers, family, and friends. It is especially problematic with parents and their children, but we will be discussing that in detail in a later chapter.

Changing dysfunctional patterns in your life is where that intelligence of your OO can help you immensely. You can shift there and, as you simply watch your thinking (rather than being your thinking); other more effective solutions will become apparent. You will see things from a higher perspective. As you practice shifting from your normal state of consciousness to this higher state, two things will happen. The first is that you will start to find the movement to being your OO becomes easier, and secondly the clarity that you experience in that state will steadily increase. Over time, you will be amazed at your capacity to see clearly what is really going on in any given situation you encounter in your life and amazed at what you missed previously.

When we are in our conditioning, we simply lack the ability to see objectively, and so all of our reactions, attempts at solutions, and decisions are based on subjective misinformation. The movement toward our OO empowers us to begin seeing reality more and more clearly. This is, in part, how you will gradually increase your level of consciousness. The other way it will happen occurs much like in any other learning situation. Someone further along in this curriculum that is capable of seeing what you may not, will offer their view. This will allow you to see various situations through their eyes, which, when you are in your OO will greatly accelerate your awareness and learning. This tutoring coupled with you in your OO will enable you to see for yourself, all of that which would normally go unnoticed.

You will know when you are regaining the capacity to experience your OO when you find yourself in a familiar situation and see that your conditioning wants you to react in the same old way, but there will be a pause. Perhaps only for a moment, but you will be able 'see' rather than 'be' the conditioning. Moments later, you may find yourself swept up in the old behavior, but something very important will have happened. Just the fact that you had that moment, that pause, made you stronger. And the next time this situation occurs, you will be even more capable of freeing yourself from that automatic response. And stronger still the next time until eventually—and this is huge—YOU and not the conditioning, will get to decide how you react. **This is the beginning of real freedom.**

There are techniques to help you speed this process along if you wish to use them. The first involves our old friend the brain. With the modern technology available they have been able to show that when someone actually performs an activity certain specific parts of the brain become active. What is not common knowledge is that when someone just imagines doing that very same activity, the exact same areas of the brain become stimulated. In other words, the brain responds to our imagining something is happening exactly as it does when we are really doing it. This knowledge is very valuable to us in our quest to become free of our conditioning.

Let's say there is a situation that occurs with some regularity between you and your significant other, a situation which normally results in your becoming frustrated and eventually angry. Assuming that you are motivated to change this interaction because you understand that if you don't, it will continue countless times in the future, and also because you know that this particular situation and others like it are seriously eroding the quality of your relationship. Utilizing this new information about how your brain functions you will begin to have the power to start changing those old interactive patterns.

Here is how you would begin. You could find a quiet moment when you would not be disturbed. The next step—and this is very important—is to access your OO. Then you would actually picture in your mind the scenario mentioned previously. As you began to re-experience it, your brain would then begin to react the way it normally does at those times and the feelings associated with this event would begin to arise. But now, in your OO, you would strongly visualize yourself reacting without frustration or anger, just observing. This strong visualization would then begin to literally change what was happening in your brain and body.

Because you would be doing this exercise with your OO, the brain would begin to dampen the normal intense responses and instead respond in a calmer way. You would have begun to change your brain and the conditioning existing there. And each time you did this exercise you would change it again. After practicing this technique for even a short time, you would notice something very interesting. The next time the situation occurs for real, you would find yourself able to exercise more control over the conditioning and, in time, your new more relaxed, more conscious response would replace your former, less effective behavior.

There is, however, one thing missing in order for this DNM technique to actually work... understanding. It would be important for you to understand that the irritation and anger you feel at these moments is simply you reacting automatically from your conditioning. It is not really about the other person. Any feelings you may experience such as judgment about their behavior, ideas of their being guilty of something, or blaming them would need to be discarded. It would be important for you to realize that this has been your automatic response to this and similar conditions, and that you have the option (because you are in your OO) to act from a more conscious and objective place.

As you do this, your focus would shift from yourself and what you were feeling to a greater awareness of what the other person was experiencing at that time. It would be necessary for you to understand that whatever they do that normally upsets you, is simply them responding to their conditioning and not take it personally. Examples of this seeing the other person might include the realization that your wife actually suffers from feelings of being unattractive and so is compelled to spend an excessive amount of time trying to look better before going out. Your ability to see this would give you compassion for her, understanding that she was in an anxious state and trying to deal with it the best she could. You might even decide to help by telling her how attractive you think she is and comforting her.

Another example of this type of seeing might be that the other person in this situation gets angry with you at times, without your knowing why. By observing this situation from your OO and shifting your focus to their feelings rather than your own it might allow you to see that the source of their anger resulted from an over critical attitude they have about themselves that they project on to you in these moments. And you will feel compassion because you would realize they have this conditioning as a result of someone in their childhood who was overly critical with them and that it is frequently making them (suffer) feel they are inadequate.

The list of possible examples is endless. What is really important to understand is that when someone is in a negative state and angry, or obsessing about how they look, or criticizing you, or whatever else they might be doing...that they are doing it unconsciously, it is not about you, and that it is something that causes them to suffer repeatedly throughout their life. You don't have to participate in the suffering by allowing their negativity to touch you and draw you down into your own conditioning.

When you start approaching your interactions with others from this higher level of consciousness, you begin to change everything. Instead of an angry dance where they react automatically from their conditioning and you do the same, and in the end both of you wind up unhappy, you will see more and more the source of their unhappy state. Then, instead of making it worse, you now have the capacity to actually begin to help them and possibly, over time, actually enable them to let go of this behavior. This type of response will always bring you closer to the other person (it will feel like—and actually be—love), rather than a conditioned response which will create more distance between you and always increase your suffering.

Your capacity for this type of seeing will increase as you become ever more capable of shifting to your OO. This has to become a state that is immediately accessible. One must become very familiar with it. Over time, your experience of this state will become increasingly profound. Not only will your ability to see what is happening at any given moment continue to increase, but so will your ability to feel what is happening with others. *At some point, you actually begin to sense what could never normally be seen.* You will be amazed at the patterns of behavior and connections that seem to unfold before you, that previously went unnoticed.

So how then to develop our capacity to shift to our OO whenever we want? One starts by finding a quiet place, and this is very important, leaving the mind entirely out of the process. You simply allow yourself to *feel* what it's like to be in your OO again. After you have achieved some success at this, the next step is to practice this same exercise at other moments in your life—right in the middle of life. One technique that works very well is to practice it whenever someone is talking to you. Instead of thinking about what you would rather be doing, did earlier, will be doing later, critiquing what they are saying or anything else, you simply allow yourself to shift to your OO and let go of any interest in any thoughts which may come to you while the other person is speaking.

Remember, the right side of our brain (the more conscious part) becomes most active during the process of learning. So you can use this period of being in your OO to 'learn' everything possible about the person you are listening to. You can be in this learning mode, simply by observing and getting yourself as far out of the way as possible.

Your mind and whatever thinking it wants to do in these moments will only impede your progress. Just be there and see what you would normally miss. What eye patterns do you see, what facial expressions are you noticing, is there a change in skin tone that occurs at times, what about the changes that may be occurring in their voice?

At first you will find yourself wandering back to thoughts of this or that, but with practice you will begin to see a great deal that you would have missed before. The way to know if you are slipping out of your OO is if you find your mind wandering, if you find yourself in any form of judgment about this person, or if you feel the need to take issue with anything they are saying.

Remember your OO looks without evaluation, without judgment. It is just seeing what is. That's the ultimate goal. When you have become proficient at this, you are well on your way. The greatest measuring stick for your progress will be when—because of what you are now able to see—you feel, not your normal conditioned response to those you come in contact with, but begin to have more compassion as you truly see the suffering they experience because of their conditioning.

First, you reestablish contact with your OO in a place of peace and quiet. Then, once you are capable of doing that quickly and easily you begin attempting to shift to your OO in various life situations whenever you feel that your, or someone else's conditioning is creating a problem. Gradually your view of yourself will change. You will start to see, little by little, your true self and become increasingly able to sculpt your personality as you wish. You will begin to be able to finally free yourself from dysfunctional patterns and experience more and more peace in your life.

There is a pitfall that one can fall into here if you are not careful. Instead of viewing themselves from their OO, they view themselves from another part of their conditioning. There is a tendency to be identified with parts of your conditioning you feel are good and consider other parts less so. For instance, someone may believe that the part of themselves that works very hard is good and the other part of them that wants to take it easy is bad. So they make the mistake of thinking they are being in their OO when they are really just in one extreme of their conditioning (the part that works very hard) watching the other.

This kind of observing is not observing at all and is of no use. Our goal is to avoid 'being' any of our conditioning, no matter how much we may like it. It is absolutely essential that this tendency is watched for very carefully and avoided. The only observations that will be of any use must come from your OO.

Earlier we discussed how our memory develops. How we start life with only implicit memory, which allows us to learn procedures like tying our shoes or riding a bike. Then around the age of eighteen months, we begin developing explicit memory, which enables us to begin storing facts and information.

You may be wondering why our memory develops in this way. This happens because in order for our explicit memory to function it requires a part of the brain called the Hippocampus. It allows us to store memories (or not) and also plays a crucial role in memory retrieval. This is the reason many people cannot recall their early childhood; the hippocampus wasn't sufficiently formed to allow for those experiences to be stored in their long-term memory. The maturing of this part of your brain continues until it's finally complete around the age of seven. In order to truly comprehend your or another person's behavior, it is absolutely essential to understand the role of the hippocampus and the dramatic effect it has in determining, not only what, but how we remember.

When we recall a memory later in life, after our hippocampus has fully developed, we have a sense of recalling something. We realize that there is our self, and that we are having this memory from our past. This is because the memory is being retrieved with the help of the hippocampus. This is how explicit memory works. However, when we experience an implicit only memory the situation is very different.

I will use the example of the battered child mentioned earlier. As an adult, when he has an implicit only memory, there is no sense of him remembering something from the past. He will not be separate from the memory and observing it. Instead, his body gets flooded with the feelings he felt during the original trauma. Rather than seeing the memory, he will actually experience those terrible emotions again. That is, his muscles will tighten, he will feel a sense of terror and dread, his body will begin producing all of the 'fight or flight' chemicals, he may begin to tremble, and he will have little or no control over these involuntary bodily responses. This is not something he is separate from and observing, it's something he is experiencing. Even though his abusive parents may be very far away, he will feel just as he did when they abused him.

This exact same process can occur with other types of trauma as well. For instance, let's look at a situation where there is a young girl whose parents were very threatening and often made her feel that she was bad and not worth loving. Picture, if you will, this small child after a bout of verbal abuse and intimidation, sobbing, feeling unloved and worthless. When this girl grows up and becomes a woman, she will be vulnerable to regressing to that same state again with all the associated emotions.

Should someone do or say something, which triggers that conditioning now stored in her implicit memory, you would no longer see a grown woman capable of responding objectively to whatever criticism she had received. Instead, you would see the same sad little girl (now with a grown up body) reacting exactly as she did when she was young, sobbing and feeling worthless.

What's important to understand is that because this is an implicit only memory that does not get processed through the hippocampus she has no warning that it is about to happen, no way to see it coming, she just suddenly finds herself in this awful state with virtually no capacity to alter her response. No amount of conversation will change how she feels and no attempt to reason with her will bring her out of that place. *You can't reach an implicit memory with explicit conversation.* You can't just tell someone that they don't need to, or should stop feeling afraid or worthless and expect them to do it. This is another reason why traditional talk therapy so often fails to achieve the desired results.

To make the situation worse, there is another area of the brain that shuts down during trauma as well, called the Broca's area, the region responsible for speech. As a result, many people experience what could be called "speechless terror." That is, they become trapped in a state where they can only continue feeling these terrible emotions, completely unable to share what they are feeling with words or even formulate any thoughts related to them.

There are countless examples of this type of conditioning occurring in people where someone suddenly begins to feel terribly insecure, angry, depressed, anxious, etc. Perhaps you have experienced something like this yourself. *Almost everyone does to some degree.*

There is another way we can be very easily led into a dark place. It has to do with the way our brain always tries to makes sense of what the body feels. Every one of us has experienced times when we were children lying in bed in the dark when we *felt* afraid. Our minds have to give us some way to process these feelings of fear, so it comes up with something for us to be afraid of, like a monster in the closet, or a boogieman coming to get us.

What's essential to understand is that the thoughts which result from the feelings in our body have nothing to do with reality. It is just our brain attempting to process those feelings. This exact same situation can occur when we are adults. Let's take the example of someone conditioned as a child to feel worthless. There might be some small thing that happened during our day where they made a mistake or felt they should have done something better. It's quite possible that this person's body will use this as an opportunity to re-experience the feeling he or she had as a child.

The body would begin to feel those feeling of worthless and inadequacy and then the mind would begin to construct thoughts to support those feelings. Soon this person would be caught in that feedback loop mentioned earlier between the body and their mind and find themselves lost in their conditioning feeling very bad about themselves.

If this same person could begin observing themselves from their OO and understand that the negative thoughts they are having about themselves are actually being generated by their body's need to re-experience those sad feelings and have nothing to do with their life now, they could begin to let go of them. They would become aware more quickly that their body was starting to feel a certain way and could relate the resultant thoughts to those feelings. They would see this situation for what it truly was. Viewing this experience from this higher place of awareness would allow them to start to break this unconscious stimulus/response and not get pulled down into it so easily, and in time, not at all.

The same thing can happen with other emotions as well. Consider the case of someone on their way to an appointment who is running late. Should they find themselves behind someone who is not in a hurry and driving at or even below the speed limit, their body will react with feelings of anger and frustration. The thoughts that follow would cause them to see the person in front of them in a very negative way and possibly result in their honking their horn, tailgating and even shouting obscenities.

Someone whose conditioning causes them to feel insecure will find that some situation occurs which causes them (their body) to feel insecure, possible because their significant other has to work late, or for some other similar reason. They will begin to think in a way that is—not necessarily consistent with reality—but rather consistent with what their body has been conditioned to feel.

You can see from this conditioned response where 'the body feels, then the mind reacts, often irrationally, that we can be driven to behavior that causes us, and possibly others, to suffer needlessly. We could allow these unconscious responses to life to continue, or we could begin to look for situations, using our OO, in our life where they occur.

Then we could, from this higher perspective and with our new understanding of what is really happening, begin to become increasingly aware of what our body was feeling. And realize the resultant thoughts are simply the product of those conditioned feelings and understand they have nothing to do with what is actually happening in the present moment. Seeing them in this way would enable us to reduce the power they held over us previously and eventually they would fade further and further away. By doing this, we would have eliminated all of the countless times in the future we would have suffered otherwise.

Understanding how these mechanisms work in others, without their conscious choice, you will feel differently the next time you see someone who appears to you to be overreacting to some situation. You will understand that they have no control over this behavior. And your knowledge that this incident is but one of many they have had, and that they will continue suffering in this same way throughout their life will give you compassion for them and help you keep from having some negative conditioned response yourself.

So what can be done to help someone who suffers uselessly in this way? We have a technique called Conscious Neuroplastic Mediation described in the next chapter which can be quite effective. But understanding the cause—*that there is some unresolved trauma in the implicit memory, which has never been integrated into the explicit memory*—tells us what must be done to heal this condition.

It is the hippocampus which aids us in integrating implicit and explicit memories and allows this healing to occur. As it turns out, the hippocampus becomes activated when we are paying attention or focused on something, *the very thing that happens when you are in your OO*. So what do we do? By giving ourselves permission to intentionally recall those traumatic moments—while in our OO—we allow the hippocampus to convert those implicit experiences into explicit memories. As this occurs, we will become increasingly able to revisit those memories without the implicit activation of our emotions.

During your review of these past experiences, you will tend to notice only what is happening in your mind such as the thoughts and images which appear. It is important that your awareness also include what's happening with your body and any sensations you may experience. This healing process must include all of you, your thoughts, your brain (which includes your entire nervous system) and your body.

Before you would have moved away from these experiences, but now, with the help of your OO, which will allow you to see rather than be this conditioning, and which activates the hippocampus, you will have the power to work toward and resolve them. It is very important for this process to happen slowly so as you begin recalling whatever traumatic event happened, you can do so without re-experiencing the negative emotions normally associated with it. Only go so far each time as you are able without being touched by what you see. This is crucial, as is remaining in your OO the entire time.

Not only does the hippocampus enable us to store long-term memories, it can also prevent it. One of its functions is to protect us. It does this during moments of extreme stress or trauma by shutting down and not allowing whatever is happening to be stored in our long-term memory. A very mild version of this can be seen when we meet someone for the first time if we are very nervous. Our body gets flooded with a stress hormone, the hippocampus becomes slightly impaired, and we find that we can't remember the name of our new acquaintance even though they just told us. And, should we experience something extreme, even as adults, we can store implicit only memories and develop unresolved trauma such as what happens to veterans during war, victims of assault and various types of accidents, etc.

This information will help you with the next step, which is to become steadily more aware of the conditioning of those around you. Seeing that they are acting from their conditioning and suffer as a result will help you to let go of the natural tendency toward judgment and move toward greater empathy and compassion. It is absolutely essential that you begin to develop the capacity to see other people and how their conditioning is running them. We will be discussing lots of examples in this book, and many more are available on the Audio Insights located on our website. After a period of studying these examples, life will become your ultimate teacher, but first a very solid foundation must be laid.

At Dynamic Neuroplastic Mediation we offer many additional techniques, which do not lend themselves to the print. Some are very powerful ways for releasing emotions, which have been stored in the body for many years, allowing one to finally become free of their negative effects. Additionally there are healing methods, which we have found can often cure almost any type of emotional problem including phobias, and usually accomplish this within minutes. Finally, there are techniques for significantly improving or even curing physical ailments such as most forms of physical pain, migraines, diabetes, circulatory problems, arthritis, ulcers, and many other diseases. Some of these are available on our website www.dynamicnm.com and others only through phone or personal consultations. Our goal—what we are most passionate about—is to significantly reduce the amount of suffering in the world, both emotional and physical.

Eight - The Quickening, Fact or Fiction?

"In times of profound change, the learners inherit the earth, while the learned find themselves beautifully equipped to deal with a world that no longer exists." ~ Eric Hoffer

Just as with the last Quickening, if you had told people about the sudden changes that were about to occur in their world, there would have been those—probably lots of those—who would have simply found it impossible to believe. No doubt, the same situation will occur now. People's reaction to this idea of a Quickening will tend to fall into one of three general categories. There will be those who have begun to feel it and for whom no reassurance is necessary. Then there will be others who perhaps have not yet felt it, but, on some level know that it's true and are highly motivated to begin learning about and employing the consciousness raising techniques we and others are teaching. Finally, there will be those who would like to believe, but remain skeptical. The idea that somehow the entire population is being lifted to a higher level of consciousness will seem implausible to them. They wonder how something like this could really be happening and if there is any proof showing that it's even possible. Fortunately, there is. What follows will show how, though we all appear to be separate from each another, we are in fact all connected.

Our planet earth is surrounded by an electromagnetic sphere that has been directly affecting all living things since life first appeared. This electromagnetic field permeates and plays a vital role in all life on the planet. This field constantly varies in strength and consistency, and with this variance, so too does life on the planet change. Each of our brains also produces an electromagnetic field, which extends beyond our bodies. Our own body's magnetic frequencies and bio-field patterns react to these changes in the

Earth's field. Recently, discoveries have been made showing that all living things sense and derive information from this natural electromagnetic field of the earth.

Without exception, all matter on Earth participates in creating this field and becomes charged with this magnetic resonance. That is, absorbs and transmits certain frequencies, not unlike the way a radio receiver does. It is important to realize that each individual cell—as well as your entire organism—senses and receives information from the natural cycles of the earth's electromagnetic field and that all electromagnetic fields carry energy (information).

The Earth has natural frequencies that are referred to as the *Schumann resonances.* The human brain also has its natural frequencies. The four basic brain waves are the Delta, Theta, Alpha, and Beta which make up the EEG, which is short for electroencephalogram and also electroencephalograph. The electroencephalograph is the recording device that produces the electroencephalogram. Each of these four brain waves is a slightly different oscillating electrical voltage in the brain. As it turns out the earth's Schuman resonances are in tune with the human brain's alpha and theta states.

The earth's electromagnetic field has an average pulse of ten cycles per second, which is referred to as the Rhythm of the Earth. One might wonder if it is just a coincidence that the brain when relaxed (in the Alpha or Theta state) is in sync with the Earth's Rhythms. What this actually shows, is how our bodies have learned to adapt to, and become in tune with, this invisible electromagnetic field.

The pineal gland, a tiny, pinecone-shaped structure in the exact center of the head has been found to respond to the earth's electromagnetic field, and controls the moods and sleeping habits of the body. It produces an enormous number of chemical substances which affect all of the other glands in the body as well as hormones which regulate the level of function of the brain.

In recent years millions of very tiny crystals have been discovered in the human body, including the brain. These crystals are made of magnetite which is the most magnetic substance known to man and is biologically unique because it is both ferromagnetic (exhibit extremely high magnetic permeability) and conducts electricity like metal. This means that it interacts strongly with magnetic and electric fields, such as that of the Earth.

We now know that there are electromagnetic fields generated by the heart that permeate every cell in the body and communicate with them transmitting information in a manner similar to radio waves. And that this energy is not only transmitted internally to the brain but *is also detectable by others within its range of communication.* The electromagnetic component of the heart's field, which is approximately 5,000 times stronger than that produced by the brain, is not impeded by tissues (like the skull which encases our brain) and can be measured several feet away from the body with a superconducting quantum interference device (SQUID)-based magnetometer.

Research in the relatively new discipline of Neurocardiology has confirmed that the heart, rather than just being an incredibly efficient pump, is much more intelligent than previously thought. In fact, it is actually a sensory organ and acts as a sophisticated information encoding and processing center that enables it to learn, remember, and make independent decisions that do not involve the brain. They have discovered neurons identical to those in the brain exist in the heart as well.

Additionally, numerous experiments have demonstrated that patterns of cardiac input to the brain not only affect autonomic regulatory centers (those parts of our nervous system that control all of the body's functions which occur automatically), but also influence higher brain centers involved in perception and emotional processing. It has also been discovered that there is a ring of neurons around our intestines, which communicates with the brain and is responsible for what is commonly called a 'gut feeling.'

It has been found that when we experience negative emotions such as anger, frustration, or anxiety, our heart rhythms become erratic and disordered, and causes our autonomic nervous system (ANS) to attempt to both stimulate and relax us at the same time, which creates great stress in our body and predisposes us to illness. At these times, the part of our ANS responsible for our 'fight or flight' response (the sympathetic nervous system) is acting in direct conflict with the part that is responsible for helping us to feel calm and relaxed (the parasympathetic nervous system). In contrast, sustained positive emotions, such as appreciation, love, or compassion are associated with highly ordered or *coherent* patterns in the heart rhythms, reflecting greater compatibility between the two branches of the ANS and a shift in autonomic balance toward increased parasympathetic (calming, relaxed) activity. This coherent state builds up rather than breaks down the body and improves the functioning of our immune system.

An important concept to understand for those wanting to exercise more control over the state of their body, and as a result their health, is the concept of coherence. There are actually several terms for this such as "Personal Coherence, and "Psychophysiological Coherence," but they all refer to the same thing, a synchronization, or harmonious working together, of our mental, physical, and emotional systems. When someone is upset, agitated, irritated, or angry, these systems are no longer in sync and when this happens, we function at a lower level than we would otherwise. Our thinking is less clear, we are less conscious, and our emotions tend to run away with us. On the other hand, when we are performing optimally, those moments when we feel more conscious and capable, it's because all of the rhythms of our body, the brain, the heart, etc. are all acting in harmony with each other, or coherent.

While coherence can occur naturally during sleep or deep relaxation, it is rare that someone is able to sustain this state for any length of time during their normal daily activities. However, research has shown that individuals can, not only create, but maintain coherence by actively generating and sustaining positive emotions. *You will discover that being in your OO will enable your body to be coherent more frequently and forever increasing durations. This will result from your beginning to feel fewer negative emotions and instead more positive ones, like compassion and love.*

The benefits to the body include significant blood pressure reduction, more efficient functioning of the heart and entire cardiovascular system, a decrease in anxiety and depression, improvement of health for individuals with diabetes or asthma, a greater sense of well-being, and a reduction in the need for medication for those suffering from conditions such as cardiac arrhythmias, chronic fatigue, fibromyalgia, and chronic pain. And finally, an increase in cognitive performance, mental clarity, and an increase in your ability to sense what others are feeling. As you develop your capacity for being in your OO, *your intuitive ability will become increasingly stronger*.

So how does this ability for intuition—to know without knowing how you know—function you might ask. And no doubt you are wondering what exactly is the mechanism by which it works, and why most people aren't able to experience it naturally? It has to do with our once again becoming sensitive to and allowing ourselves to see that which is there, but which we have simply lost our capacity to perceive.

Our normal perceptions of what we see are provided by information such as an objects shape, color, and/or function. But what we are not usually aware of is the additional information coming to us on another level. It takes specialized training for an individual to be able to perceive this data. One example of this type of training is developing your capacity to go deeply into your OO. There is enormous evidence suggesting that the brain has these capabilities at birth, but unfortunately, they get suppressed by conditioning in childhood and lack of practice. This is what causes us to lose the natural ability for greater conscious and intuitive perceptions as we begin, more and more, to utilize primarily our left-brain.

Especially here in the west, educational focus has been primarily on the left-brain and rational functions rather than developing right brain intuitive functions. However, psychics and mystics consistently demonstrate that it is possible to regain this capacity by focusing our attention and quieting the left-brain—both of which occur when you are in your OO. This is how you will begin to allow these intuitive perceptions to appear.

As to the mechanism enabling these intuitive perceptions, the previous explanation showing how we are all able to communicate via the Earth's electromagnetic field provides part of the answer. Quantum mechanics (QM), gives another. QM is a set of principles which describe physical reality at the atomic and subatomic level of matter and Quantum theory is at the cornerstone of every natural science from physics, chemistry, biology and cosmology. It explains everything from why the stars shine to how photosynthesis works and is at the root of all biological processes. It even explains how our universe came to exist.

Almost all modern technologies are based on devices developed using the principles of quantum mechanics. More importantly, Quantum theory is said to be the single most accurate explanation ever developed for describing reality. It describes all of the interactions between energy and matter in the universe, including Zero-Point Energy (ZPE), which is an almost unlimited energy source that permeates and sustains all matter and exists everywhere (even in the vacuum of outer space) and *allows for the transmission of information as patterns of energy*.

It has also been discovered, during attempts to improve functional Magnetic Resonance Imaging (fMRI) that when there is an emission of energy from one source that gets absorbed by another, that energy carries with it information about the original object.

This energy contains atomic particles which are said to be entangled and they continuously emit (broadcast) non-locally and are received by and interact with the other entangled particle pair in its environment through a subtle process involving this exchange of information. This is an extension of the process know as quantum emission/absorption and similar to non-local quantum entanglement.

Quantum entanglement proposes that all things in the universe are interconnected and exchange information by way of these entangled particles. It also maintains that underlying this unity or oneness is the interaction between all matter, energy and information. These processes give us a way to understand how the whole of creation is capable of learning, self-correcting, and evolving as a self-organizing inter-connected holistic system that is capable of becoming more conscious, as is happening now with the Quickening.

What we have discussed so far shows how, though we appear completely separate from each other, in fact, each and every one of our bodies electromagnetic fields are affecting and constantly being affected by the earth's electromagnetic field. And even though we cannot see it with the naked eye, we are all continually bathed in it. A field with which we are all communicating constantly and *that allow us to communicate with each other*.

Each of our own electromagnetic fields can directly influence others close to us. And because we are constantly communicating with the Earth's electromagnetic field (as is every living thing on the planet) we are all essentially connected to each other. What you are going to read next is an example of how this communication can be used to create significant changes in the population in general.

What I am about to describe is one of the most dramatic sociological experiments ever conducted. In 1993, a group of researchers predicted in advance that the calming influence of group meditation practice could reduce violent crime by over 20 percent in Washington, D.C., during an 8-week period in the summer of that year.

As it turns out, the results were even greater than expected, the rate of violent crime—which included assaults, murders, and rapes—decreased by 23 percent during the June 7 to July 30 experimental period. *It's important to note here that those people who would have committed those crimes, but didn't, were somehow moved away from violence—that is toward greater consciousness, without ever knowing this was happening to them.* And those who might suggest that it was a chance occurrence should know that the odds of this happening are less than 2 in 1 billion. And rigorous statistical analyses ruled out an extensive list of alternative explanations.

The project involved assembling nearly 4,000 practitioners of the Transcendental Meditation and TM-Sidhi programs from over 80 countries who were brought to D.C. and housed throughout the city. John Hagelin, lead author of the study and director of the Institute of Science, Technology and Public Policy says previous research had shown that these meditation techniques "create a state of deep relaxation and coherence in the individual and simultaneously appear to produce an effect that spreads into the environment, *influencing people who are not practicing the techniques and who have no knowledge of the experiments themselves.*"

Drawing on terminology from quantum field theories, Hagelin, an eminent physicist, refers to the findings as a field effect of consciousness. He says, "It's analogous to the way that a magnet creates an invisible field that causes iron filings to organize themselves into an orderly pattern. Similarly, these meditation techniques have been shown to create high levels of coherence in EEG brain wave patterns of individual practitioners. This increased coherence and orderliness in individual consciousness appears to spill over into society and can be measured indirectly via changes in social behavior, such as reductions in the rate of violent crime."

This experiment was rigorously analyzed by a 27-member project review board composed of independent scientists and civic leaders who approved the research protocol and monitored the research process. *And to date, there have actually been more than 42 similar studies conducted during the past 25 years all verifying this same consciousness raising effect.*

One of the things that make the Washington, D.C., experiment especially significant is that the predictions were lodged in advance with a panel of prominent social scientists and civic leaders, including members of the District city council and metropolitan police force. Statistical analysis considered the effect of weather variables, daylight, police patrolling, historical crime trends and annual patterns in the District of Columbia, as well as trends in neighboring cities.

Popular opinion has always been that we can reduce violence with more police, greater gun control, stiffer penalties, etc. But, the fact that violence and crime continue to be a major problem in our society, makes it obvious that these approaches are simply inadequate. However new this idea of The Quickening may be, evidence consistently shows that it can raise the consciousness of those affected and reduce, not only violent crime, but the general level of negativity within the population.

We have always thought of our consciousness as being completely separate from others with no common field linking us together. But the latest scientific discoveries we have been discussing have shown this notion is completely false.

There are, in fact, many examples of one person influencing the physical state of another at a distance. Many researchers have clearly shown that humans are not only capable of highly accurate long-range awareness of local details and events but they are also capable of affecting the health of others at distant locations. For example, a great deal of data is now available showing that both Qigong masters and adepts can significantly influence materials both close to them as well as at great distances.

Physics has shown us that any flowing electrical current produces a magnetic field in the space around it (as does the earth), and that a changing, pulsing, or moving magnetic field can produce an electrical current flow in an electrical conductor placed within that field (such as our brains). In other words, ***the electrical activity of each of our brains individually and collectively is affecting and being affected by each other via the earth's magnetic field,*** we are changing and being changed by it all the time.

What is crucial to understand is that magnetic and electromagnetic fields have energy and can carry information. *The energy fields of humans, plants, animals, the earth, and the universe provide the interface that connects us all.* Thus explaining how the Quickening that is happening now is capable of affecting each and every one of us without our even knowing it.

An individual or especially a very special group of conscious individuals can become the equivalent of a transmitter of higher consciousness in the same way that a television or radio transmitter stimulates the electromagnetic field in a specific manner and then transmits waves through the field that can be picked up at a distance. The experiment in D.C. is a perfect example of this and has shown us that a group of people who are able to create a very coherent state within their own bodies are not only able to influence, but in fact, increase the coherence of many others many miles away. That is, bring them to a higher state of consciousness and functioning.

According to David Edwards, professor of government at the University of Texas at Austin, this research and the theory behind it deserve the most serious consideration. He said, "I think the claim can be plausibly made that the potential impact of this research exceeds that of any other ongoing social or psychological research program. It has survived a broader array of statistical tests than most research in the field of conflict resolution. This work and the theory that informs it deserve the most serious consideration by academics and policy makers alike."

This Quickening is happening and will change our world forever. Next, we will discuss how you can begin to experience it for yourself.

Nine - Additional DNM Techniques for Tapping into The Quickening.

"Meditation in the MIDST of action is a billion times superior to meditation in stillness." ~ Hakuin Ekaku, revered as one of the greatest teachers in the history of Japanese Zen.

As I describe below the changes that one undergoes as they are affected by the Quickening you may find yourself asking, "Are you being touched by this Quickening without even being aware of it?" Could that happen? Yes, it is quite possible that you are and not even know it. The change in your feelings can happen so subtly that they may go completely unnoticed.

We have discussed how the first step is to access your OO and from that place of higher consciousness begin observing yourself and then others. For those who do this, they will discover for themselves things they could never have imagined otherwise. They will begin to see themselves and others as they actually are, rather than through the foggy lens of their conditioning. It is no exaggeration to say that the quality of their life will increase significantly in direct proportion to the amount of time they spend separating themselves from their conditioning and being their OO.

There are other things you can do to accelerate the process if you wish. One is by exchanging these ideas with others whom you feel would be receptive. When you do this, there is a synergistic effect that occurs and the more people involved, the greater the force of that effect.

It is our conditioned thoughts, which fuel the negative states. Consider how angry you would be if you never had an angry thought, or how lonely you would be if you never had a thought about being lonely. Normally, the stream of thoughts begins and, try as we might, we can't seem to stop them and get pulled in deeper and deeper. What is needed at these moments is a way to cut off the fuel supply (the negative thoughts) feeding the negative emotions. But how?

What usually happens when someone begins this process is that they start to struggle with each negative thought in an attempt to push it away. The energy involved in trying to separate from a negative thought actually causes the opposite to happen. It is as if, when we push in one direction, There will be a corresponding reaction of moving in the opposite direction. That is why it never works well, or for long.

What is needed instead is *neither going with, nor trying to stop the thought.* Instead, we just sort of surrender and let go of it. It is like letting a stone drop from your hand. Holding it requires more energy than simply relaxing and letting it fall. If you begin to try this, you will find that in time, this technique works quite well in learning to manage your thoughts.

It is important to realize that thoughts by themselves have absolutely no power; it is when we allow them to become emotionally charged that they begin to affect us. This 'simply letting go' divests them of any energy and they lose their power over us. Over time, as we allow them less and less energy, they will begin to dissipate and eventually disappear. You can think of the process as a continual letting go of each negative thought as it appears. The more you practice this, the better you get. Eventually you can become quite good at it and find that it is difficult for any negative emotion to take over and control you.

There is another way we can stop these thoughts dead in their tracks and raise our level of consciousness...simply by asking for it. You can replace the negative stream of thoughts by repeating the phrase "More conscious, more conscious, more conscious..." to yourself. Just by repeating that phrase in your mind over and over *with the intent of becoming more conscious* you will be able to move in that direction.

This phrase can be used anytime you feel yourself getting irritated, agitated, angry, sad, or whatever. As you continually practice this technique, your brain will literally change, and along with it, your previous conditioning, until you eventually find that your response to those situations is no longer reflexively negative. Those situations will occur but be unable to touch you. You will have eliminated all of the countless times in the future you would have normally suffered (and possibly caused others to suffer as well) had you not begun this practice.

It is important to understand that our thinking is strongly influenced by the state of our body. So another approach to moving from a lower to a higher state of consciousness is by becoming aware of your body. If you are feeling anxious or angry, check to see if your body is relaxed. You may find that your face, shoulders and other parts of your body are not. Consciously doing a walk through from your toes to your scalp and releasing any tension can often alleviate the anxiety or anger without needing to do anything else.

As you become more aware of yourself, you will notice that you have certain postures associated with each emotional state; those which you assume when you are angry, anxious, depressed, etc. You will begin to see that your body is in a certain posture connected to whatever emotion you are feeling, and that simply by changing it the associated feelings begin to dissipate rather quickly.

The more aware of your own postures and their connection to certain states, the more you will become aware of the same thing happening to others. Helping them to change their posture when in a negative state will have the same beneficial effect on them.

Exercise is another way to rid yourself of negative energy. Simply going for a walk or doing some other form of physical activity will normally burn up that energy and free you from it. Remember, the mind, the brain, and the body are each capable of affecting the other.

Be particularly aware of your breathing when you feel yourself turning negative. You will find, at these times that your breathing becomes more rapid and shallow. Your ability to see this during these moments will allow you to bring yourself to a better place just by returning to slow, deep, and relaxed breathing.

Caffeine from Coffee and soft drinks, nicotine from cigarettes, sugar from sweets, artificial coloring and many other things you ingest can dramatically alter your mood. There is a simple test you can perform on yourself to see how your body reacts to various things you put in it. This is how it works; allow yourself to go three hours without eating or drinking anything and then check your pulse. The next step is to have one thing, be it a cup of coffee or whatever, but it must be just one food or drink. After you have consumed it, wait 15 minutes for liquids and 30 minutes for everything else then check your pulse again. If you see that your heart rate has increased, you will be able to see how what you ate or drank is affecting your body.

Anything that increases your heart rate is going to affect not just your body, but also your brain and *your thoughts.* This easy test can help you identify those things you may wish to avoid in the future because you may become aware that they alter your thinking, but not in a positive way. Many people become increasingly agitated, irritated or predisposed toward anger or aggressive behavior after ingesting any type of stimulant. Through watching your own behavior from your OO, you may decide that the pleasure you associate with the consumption of whatever it is that stimulates you is not worth the resultant effects on your behavior.

It is worth noting that this same diagnostic method can be used also to check for food allergies. Any food you are allergic to will cause your heart rate to rise significantly, allowing you to easily identify it and its negative effect on your body.

Getting into the habit, of doing random acts of kindness as often as you can is another way to work toward greater consciousness. Negativity feeds on and perpetuates negativity. Not participating in negative discussions about others can reverse this process, as does allowing someone a little room to be negative without your reacting similarly. Beginning to look for ways throughout your day, where you can consider others is a wonderful way to move away from your negative conditioning; Such as letting someone go ahead of you at an intersection, doing what someone else wants rather than what you would prefer, and doing the listening exercise mentioned earlier as often as you can remember.

Consciously attempting to say something positive to someone when you see they may be in a bad place emotionally, allowing someone to say something negative and simply not reacting, trying to be more aware of what your children or your significant other's day was like and what you might do to make them feel better, all work toward lifting you up to a place of higher consciousness.

We have all had the experience of being in the fast lane on the interstate driving at or near the speed limit when suddenly someone comes flying up behind us. Next they indicate rather aggressively that they want us to move over by getting closer and closer to our car. Our conditioned response in that situation is to become irritated or angry. When we do this we can actually feel our energy increase in the area of our solar plexus, I call this 'burning.' Everyone is familiar with this sensation and the associated stream of negative thoughts that begins to reduce our level of consciousness rather severely. If we allow ourselves to become negative, we may actually slow down or just remain doggedly in the lane and not let them past, all the while continuing to 'burn,' and enjoying the fact that the person behind us is burning as well.

These moments offer us a wonderful opportunity to try something different and allow us to increase our level of consciousness. We can experiment, and instead of going with our automatic negative reaction, simply move over and let them by (or accommodate the other person in whatever way the situation calls for) and using our OO become aware of how very different this feels. Instead of burning, losing energy, having your level of consciousness decrease, and moving closer to violence, you can side step those feelings, let go, and imagine this person to be a friend whom you have decided to show some consideration. Instead of the burning, there will be a feeling of lightness. Look for every opportunity in your daily life to practice this technique. Not only will you be eliminating more and more moments in your life where you would be unhappy (burn), you will actually be having a positive influence on the person you considered as well. Kindness and consideration (being more conscious) has a rippling effect on the world in general.

A recent Gallup poll reported that motorists were more worried about road rage (42%) than about drunk driving (35%). - NY Times. The Mizell Report, commissioned by AAA, uncovered 10,037 crashes caused by violent aggressive driving between January 1, 1990 and August 31, 1996. At least 218 men, women and children were killed as a result of these incidents and another 12,610 were injured. This problem is national in scope, not just a phenomenon of congested urban areas.

Aggressive driving may be a factor in 50% of auto crashes, based on the Washington Beltway Study. Source: Analysis of the Capital Beltway Crash Problem, U.S. DOT, March 1996. The problem is getting worse according to the AAA. There has been a compound growth rate of 7%. As the Quickening touches more people and they begin practicing what we just discussed, we will start to see these statistics drop, dramatically reducing the amount of violence just related to driving.

Earlier I mention how we all develop these disparate (polar opposite) personalities growing up. Working to resolve these opposites in yourself and others is another way to speed up your development. I will give you a simple, yet highly effective technique for doing this.

Let's say that there are times when your significant other is really happy with you and then other times when he or she seems to feel very different. Instead of seeing you as a caring, loving spouse who loves them and with whom they wish to spend the rest of their life, they see you in a very different light. This will simply be them moving from one opposite within themselves to another, something triggered an implicit activation and they are revisiting a negative state, much as the people in our examples did (the battered boy and the girl who was made to feel worthless).

Perhaps when these moments occur you have tried to talk with them and reassure them you are still the same person who loves and adores them. In most cases, this type of conversation proves useless (our earlier discussion about the hippocampus, implicit, and explicit memory explains why). When someone is lost in their conditioning, experiencing an implicit emotional reaction, their ability to be objective is severely diminished. It is very difficult, and often impossible, for anything you can say at those moments to bring them back. They are reliving a negative situation from their childhood and you are at that moment simply a player (and not a very nice one) in that drama. Anything you say will be seen to come from that character's attempt to lie, or cause them more pain. What to do? We discussed how this situation can be handled in the last chapter and mentioned Conscious Neuroplastic Mediation, but not the details. Here is how it works.

You wait until they are in a place where they know that you love them and they are very happy with you. Then you ask them what is real, the feelings they have now, or the feelings they have when

91

they relive their childhood drama? They will say that they know that what they are feeling now is the truth, but when they revert to that other state, they seem to forget all of that and find themselves believing just the opposite.

The task at hand is to introduce one extreme psychological state to the other. The ideal would be if there were two of them and when they turn to feeling negative, the other version of them who knows they love you could have a conversation with the other. Obviously, this isn't possible. However, there is a way we can achieve the same effect.

While they are in a positive place, ask them make a recording (video would be best, but if not then audio) saying something like, "I know that I love my husband (or wife), that he (or she) loves me, and that I want to spend the rest of my life with him (or her)." It will be important to address each negative thing they say while in their other state, i.e. if one of the comments is "I don't trust you!", and then it will be important to have them say the opposite in the recording. Have them say that they know that sometimes they shift into a negative place and, at those times, they say things which are not really true.

Once the recording is made, you both agree that when they flip back into that negative state, that they will go and get the recording and sit and watch (or just listen) to it. There may be some resistance to this in the beginning, but with time and repeated commitments during their positive state, eventually they will do it. We also want to have an agreement that you will record the person in their negative state, which they will watch or listen to in their more positive state.

This bringing together of the opposites (your significant other seeing and hearing *themselves* act very different) in both their positive and negative states will eventually free them from this dark place. Anything anyone else says while they are in their negative state will be difficult for them to accept, but they can't ignore there own comments.

The same thing can be done to overcome polar swings in yourself. We will use a very common situation. You find yourself in a relationship that causes you great pain and know you need to break it off. Part of you understands the relationship will only cause you more and more pain and yet, at times, another part wants to rush back into it. Making a recording while you are experiencing pain where you list all of the reasons the relationship needs to end and why (preferably in your OO) and playing it when you are attempted to return for more suffering and help immensely.

So many of our goals go unrealized because of these polar states within us, one side of us literally sabotages the other. Being able to see them through the eyes of your OO and then utilizing the technique of Conscious Neuroplastic Mediation to reduce and eventually eliminate them will give you the power to change negative behaviors and attain goals never before possible. You will find many other powerful techniques for change on our web site www.dynamicnm.com.

Diligently practicing all of these techniques along with being in your OO as often as possible and seeing yourself and others from this higher place will slowly move you up the scale mentioned in the next chapter.

Ten - How to Measure Your Progress.

"Peace cannot be achieved through violence; it can only be attained through understanding." ~ Albert Einstein

How to judge your progress? How can you know that you are becoming ever freer of your conditioning and continually moving toward higher consciousness? I will now give you a way to measure your present status, a method of indicating where you are now and also how to gauge your progress. In order to do this, we have to have some sort of measuring device, a way of knowing our relative position along our path to higher consciousness.

You may be asking yourself if it is actually possible to accurately measure yourself or another person's progress. It is. There is a way to look into yourself or someone else and understand what that individual's life experience is like. How? We just need to change our perspective a little.

First we must understand that a person cannot be judged, that is to say, you cannot measure another person by how much money they have, how successful they have been in business, how attractive they are, how many people they have around them, how well they speak, or what they have read. **The only true measure of a person is the degree of effort required to turn them negative.**

Picture if you will a vertical scale measuring from 100 at the bottom, to 1 at the top. Next, imagine that the 1 at the top represents a personality similar to that of Gandhi, and that the 100 at the bottom represents the other extreme in human behavior; an individual of the meanest, cruelest, and most violent nature.

We now have our scale and with that, we can begin to see how we could indicate—depending on how quickly someone could be turned negative—where they would belong along this spectrum. We know that someone who is at the bottom of the scale would need little or no prompting to become violent and commit the most horrendous acts. Whereas someone at the top would not become angry regardless of whatever terrible thing might be done to them (i.e. Mahatma Gandhi saying *"And eye for an eye makes the whole world blind."* or Christ being crucified and saying *"Father forgive them for they know not what they do."*).

Individuals who find themselves near the bottom of our scale will be people whose lives are filled with never ending violence and pain, all of which they unknowingly bring upon themselves. At the other end is someone whose life is filled with peace, regardless of the circumstances of their external life.

Most of us fall somewhere in between these two extremes, and where we are on that scale, that is, **how quickly we can be affected by some outside stimulus to become angry,** determines how much progress we have made, and, more than anything else, the quality of our relationships, our work, and every other aspect of our life.

We can see that there would be an inverse relationship between an individual's tendency toward negativity and the amount of peace in their life. More negative, less happy. And of course, the reverse would be true, the less negative, more happy.

Before we continue, we need to take a look at another obstacle to our fully understanding and making use of this scale. It is the idea that someone can be a very nice person, but still be capable of violence in any form. This notion stems from our need to justify our violent behavior, which results from our present level of consciousness.

This theme is repeated over and over again in nearly every action movie created. See if this sounds familiar. We have a nice guy who is minding his own business. Then the bad guy or guys show up and burn his house down, beat him up, steal his woman, kick his dog, or commit some other acts of brutality which results in our good guy turning into a Rambo like character. Isn't this where the movie really becomes enjoyable? Finally, after waiting through all of that build up, we get to see what we came for, our "good" guy completely justified in committing terrible acts of violence.

This scenario allows us to enjoy violence (against those bad people) without feeling any guilt because, after all, they had it coming. I cannot help mentioning the scene in *"The Unforgiven"* with Clint Eastwood where his partner says to him (after they have killed someone) "I guess he had it coming." And Clint says, "We all have it coming."

The truth is, as long as we believe that violence is acceptable for any reason, we will always be surrounded by it as we are now. And what differentiates one person from another on our scale, is their ability to separate themselves from this notion. So, if you wish to judge yourself, to see where you are and understand what needs to be done to move up the scale, all you have to do is observe yourself in your dealings with other people. Throughout the day, do you get irritated, angry, or upset frequently, fairly regularly, or hardly ever?

We can also get a better idea of our placing by asking ourselves some hard questions. For instance, under what circumstances would it be acceptable to kill another person? What about hurting them physically? Or even wishing them harm? When, in your mind, would this be acceptable? What, to you justifies committing or envisioning violence toward another human being?

Should you ask yourself one of the above questions and find that you do not like the answer, don't be too hard on yourself. We all grow up in a very violent world. It would be difficult for you to feel otherwise. *The fear we all have is at the core of this notion of revenge. We all need to feel that we can defend ourselves against the tremendous amount of the violence we see in the world and are able to eliminate this fear, at least for a time, vicariously, by watching our 'hero' wreak havoc on the bad guys.*

We are told in church to obey the Ten Commandments, for example, Thou shalt not kill, then inducted into the military and sent off to some place like Viet Nam where we are told that we should kill, maybe even receiving a medal for it. We are also told

96

that killing is not ok, and yet we have the death penalty still imposed by many (but fortunately not all) states. And the most dramatic contradiction of all is God who said, "Thou shalt not kill" himself killing every human on earth except Noah, his wife, his sons, and their wives in the flood. And this is but one of many examples of God ordering the death of not only men, but women, children and helpless animals.

Here are just a few more of the many to be found in the Bible:

"And he smote the men of Bethshemesh, because they had looked into the ark of the LORD, even he smote of the people fifty thousand and threescore and ten men: and the people lamented, because the LORD had smitten many of the people with a great slaughter."
(I Samuel 6:19)

"Thus saith the LORD of hosts, I remember that which Amalek did to Israel, how he laid wait for him in the way, when he came up from Egypt. Now go and smite Amalek, and utterly destroy all that they have, and spare them not; but slay both man and woman, infant and suckling, ox and sheep, camel and ass."
(I Samuel 15:2-3)

"Every one that is found shall be thrust through; and every one that is joined unto them shall fall by the sword. Their children also shall be dashed to pieces before their eyes; their houses shall be spoiled, and their wives ravished." (Isaiah 13:15-16)

According to the Bible, in total God kills 371,186 people directly and orders another 1,862,265 people murdered.

Can anyone read the above quotes or the numbers that follow and not ask themselves how this could be possible? It's possible because some of those who wrote the bible projected their own hatred and anger onto God and had their own agenda, which was basically to control the masses through fear and justify everything they or their people did, including looting, murder, rape, etc.

Most people do not realize that our modern Bibles are the result of many translations; essentially copies of copies many times over and that many thousands of errors which occurred during that copying have been discovered. Or that there was a Jewish procedure where a Scribe would copy the bible and then destroy the original because they did not want there to be numerous versions where one could be compared with another so there could never be any question about which one was actually correct.

This allowed for a lot of creativity by each Scribe and shows how the details where God did such things as mention above could have easily been added over time. A current example of this type of 'creativity' in interpretation can be seen in a comment made recently by John Piper (a well known pastor and theologian) when he speculated that a tornado was a message from God urging Lutheran's not to affirm homosexuality. His comment tells us much more about his feelings than God's. Understanding that this is the procedure which resulted in our present day Bible, we can see that there is simply no possible way to ever reconstruct accurately the details of what happened on any particular day over 3,000 years ago.

If there is a God, he would have to be someone who transcends all of our human weaknesses. He would be someone at the very top of our scale, the very epitome of love and acceptance. Can you really imagine that he would be someone who would get angry, seek revenge, ask parents to sacrifice their offspring, or who would kill innocent women and children, and helpless animals?

Anyone who would do such things would belong at the very bottom of our scale. As we become more conscious we will see the complete insanity of embracing violence in any form. We will come to understand that violence is self-perpetuating and that the only way to ever begin to bring it to an end is by changing our present paradigm, and see also that the notion of God as some violent being with a quick temper that would do such horrific things as utter nonsense.

Every child who attends church or goes to Bible School grows up hearing the quotes above or others like them and simply accepts them as though somehow these obvious contradictions are somehow justified. How can it happen that most people never ask if God said "Thou Shalt Not Kill" that killing, especially by God himself, is ok? This happens because we simply take in what we hear as children and then without ever thinking about it again, continue to allow it to be part of our belief system.

We are no longer children. And no conscious adult with a rational mind who takes the time to reconsider the question "When is it ok to commit murder?" could possibly come up with any answer they would find acceptable other than "Never!"

The truth is, all of us have been getting mixed messages all of our lives, partly due to the problem of relative understanding. When the commandments were handed down there were already laws about killing other people, they always existed in some form or another. Did we really need someone to tell us again not to kill? Of course not. The Commandments where meant to be interpreted in a different way. What that Commandment actually means is that we are not supposed to kill, harm, etc. others *in our minds*. That is, we should not have harmful thoughts about others. But, because of a lack of understanding they have all been taken in the wrong way. We are told one thing, but everything we see tells us we are perfectly justified in hurting others if they are 'bad.' At some point, as someone progresses up our scale, they will let go of this notion. The only way to move up the scale is to re-examine any conditioning you may have which condones anger and violence and begin separating from it.

99

An individual's negative reaction to others can be more subtle, where one does not express their negativity overtly, but instead causes them to isolate themselves by driving others away. They decide that they would rather be alone than have to put up with anyone's nonsense.

This is just another way of saying that they lack sufficient tolerance and patience (love) toward others. They feel more irritation and anger when they are around others than they do love, and so prefer to avoid all of these other irritating and annoying people. If you stop and think about this, you will begin to understand many things more clearly. You will be able to see why it is some people have such difficulty in so many areas of their lives while others experience greater happiness.

The really tragic side to this is that most people don't realize that the problem is not 'out there' but rather within them. That when they react negatively, that it is entirely about them, and never see what this tendency has done, is doing, and will do in their lives. They always believe the source of their irritation, frustration, anger, or other negative emotions lies outside themselves. They don't see that someone else may react entirely different in the same situation, that is, without the negativity. And so they continue, like Don Quixote, fighting imaginary enemies, those people they believe are "bad," a view they create through their negative emotions.

It is possible, in fact, it often happens that someone goes through their entire life moving further and further from others, preferring their solitude and never understanding that it is simply their lack of patience, understanding, compassion, and tolerance (in a word, Love) that transforms normal situations into unhappy ones, when it doesn't have to be that way and that their life could be very different.

The answer? Utilizing the techniques of DNM to develop more tolerance, patience, and compassion for others. Only by letting go of that negative reactive conditioning and the destructive emotions which result can anyone ever improve the quality of their life. Anyone who cares to do this work will experience greater peace and happiness in direct proportion to their ability to separate themselves from their negativity. It is absolutely essential that we learn to look deep in the mirror to see the real source of our unhappiness.

Yet another example of our hearing a message but misunderstanding it is when Christ said that we must die and be born again. Again, instead of taking his words literally, what if we considered that he might have meant that it is our conditioned personality that must die, and through that experience, we will be reborn anew. Doesn't saying that we must change who we are during our life make a great deal more sense than thinking that we have to die to raise ourselves up to a higher level of consciousness?

In the process of measuring our ongoing progress a journal can be a great help. It will be important to make notes regarding what you are beginning to see about yourself and refer back to them often. You can even use it like a detective might use case notes to solve a crime. You could focus on some aspect of your behavior or your interaction with another that you are particularly interested in seeing more clearly and then keep track of your 'investigation' as it progresses.

All conditioned behavior has a negative emotional charge associated with it, that's what fuels it and binds us to it. Becoming more and more sensitive to these feelings you probably never noticed before will assist you in your ability to feel, even if you can't see, that you are acting from your conditioning.

Remember, **whenever you are feeling anger, irritation, agitation, impatience or any other negative emotions, you can be sure that you are in your conditioning.** In the beginning, you will simply find yourself, at times, in these negative states unable to do anything about it. However, by attempting to be aware of the feelings you are experiencing and reminding yourself that they are a sure sign you are in your conditioning, will begin to help you separate from them. Of course, as you become more capable of shifting to your OO whenever you want, this will allow you to pull yourself up quickly or avoid them altogether. The more you practice this, the more you—rather than your conditioning—will decide how you act.

The surest sign that you are making progress will result from the increased amount of tolerance, patience, and compassion you begin to have for others. In the beginning, you may find that more often than not you still react with anger or some other negative emotion. But gradually you will see a shift taking place where, what you see from this place of higher consciousness, results in your feeling more positive and fewer negative emotions.

Watching the actions of other people can be a great help and allow us to learn from their mistakes. When you see someone reacting to some life situation negatively, you will begin to see how mechanical their response is, how they are stuck in that behavior, are suffering from it at that moment, and will suffer from it countless times in the future. For example, when you are in your OO and see a person who gets upset repeatedly about the same type of situation and then rants on and on. Seeing this will increase your desire to do something different, to free yourself from all of the useless suffering that would await you otherwise.

Reminding yourself that no one asked for the programming that results in their feeling insecure, angry, depressed, etc. will allow you to have more compassion. Understanding that, most people become very identified with their conditioned personality, never realizing that they can change, and continue to simply believe this is just who they are will give you greater compassion for them. Any suggestion that they might want to change some aspect of their personality (even if it is causing them immense suffering) will be met with defensiveness and probably anger. They don't realize that they may not have had any say so originally, but that they most certainly could now. Seeing how they are trapped in their conditioning and how they will continue to suffer will increase your compassion for them.

Eleven - Getting Out of The Basement.

"Everyone is overridden by thoughts; that's why they have so much heartache and sorrow. At times I give myself up to thought purposefully; but when I choose, I spring up from those under its sway. I am like a high-flying bird, and thought is a gnat: how should a gnat overpower me?" ~ Rumi

There will be moments when you find yourself becoming angry, frightened, sad, anxious, depressed or feeling some other negative emotion. These feelings can range from mild to extreme, sometimes very extreme. These are states that everyone feels at times and what we have in common with all other human beings.

Our conditioning has set us up to experience these feelings and we have been given few if any tools to adequately help us in these moments. As a result, we suffer, sometimes terribly, with no way to free ourselves. As I write these words, countless people are suffering in this way and is why so many people often turn to drugs (prescription or non prescription), alcohol, or continue to live lives of quiet desperation, experiencing these feelings again and again.

From the statistics we mentioned earlier related to suicide we know that someone, in the sixteen minutes it took me to type this paragraph committed suicide, as did someone else in the previous sixteen minutes and, on average, every sixteen minutes someone else will choose to take their own life.

Some of these individuals could very likely have been spared this fate were it not for a phenomenon which occurs when someone feels a negative emotion repeatedly. They experience these emotions so often that they become used to them and as a result come to think of them as a normal part of their life, accepting that this is just how they are, will continue to be, and believe nothing can be done to help them escape the terrible pain these emotions cause them to feel.

I cannot help but wonder how many more could have been saved had they received more compassion, understanding, and love from others. You may work or come in contact with someone who is contemplating ending their life and never realize it until after it has happened. And if you just met them in passing, you probably would never have sensed their pain or known that this was the last day of their life.

The truth is, we should all be, at least most of the time, enjoying our lives. If you feel negative emotions frequently, it is important for you to understand that this is not the way it has to be. The quality of your life could be vastly different. If you have begun to watch yourself from your OO, you may have already become aware of some of these feelings and see them more clearly than before. This is a very important step; to watch yourself from your OO for those moments when you begin slipping into some negative state. If you aren't even consciously aware that it is happening, that is, if you are completely lost in being that conditioning, rather than seeing that conditioning, it will be much more difficult, if not impossible for you to deal with or change.

Still, in the beginning and possibly for some time, you will find yourself on occasion in some dark place feeling very upset, suffering, and need a way out. From our earlier discussions you know that it is likely that your body has become very used to feeling these negative emotions (in fact, addicted to them) and that any attempt to move away from them will be met with strong resistance.

We have all witnessed this reluctance to give up feeling negative when we encounter a friend in a bad place and try to help them. You can talk to them, reassure them, and offer logical reasons why they shouldn't be feeling the way they do, yet they continue to suffer. Perhaps you have even noticed this tendency in yourself when you are in a negative state and someone else tries to bring you out of it.

If we can begin to observe these moments through the eyes of our OO we will start to see that some part of us (our conditioning) actually wants to continue experiencing those feelings. This is an extremely important observation, because if you don't see this resistance for what it is and just go with it, there is little that anyone can do to help. You have to understand clearly, what is going on, that you are split at those moments. There is the part of you that wants the suffering to stop and another, often more powerful part of yourself that drives you to continue.

This awareness is the way out because it will allow you to make efforts that would otherwise be impossible. And each time you make those efforts, that part of you that wants to move away from suffering will become stronger and stronger. Let me say it again, as long as you are lost in the conditioning which is the true cause of your suffering and unable to do anything but be that conditioning, you will unconsciously sabotage any efforts to change your state. However, if you can separate yourself from it, even a little bit, then this will enable you to begin to employ the methods which follow.

The particular technique or techniques you apply will vary depending on which negative emotion you are experiencing as well as its intensity. We will start with the example of someone experiencing agitation or mild anger. The first step would be, as always, for them to try to move to their OO to whatever extent they are able. This would allow them to see, if only slightly, their conditioning occurring. The extent to which they were able to do this would determine entirely the degree to which they were able to make any real efforts to change their state.

The next step would be for them to become aware of what was happening with their body and breathing. Intentionally relaxing their body from head to foot would begin to help, as would allowing their breathing to become slower and deeper. Then they would focus on their solar plexus (the place where what I refer to

106

as 'the burn' is felt when one gets angry) and consciously feel a strong sense of gratitude or love emanating from that area. Continuing this process for several minutes is often enough to alleviate both irritation and anger.

After doing the above, should you find yourself still having difficulty letting go of the conditioned anger, you could begin (if you are not driving or something similar) an alternate tapping of your left hand on your left thigh then your right hand on your right thigh. This technique works extremely well in resolving states of agitation and anger because it creates an alternate activation of the right and then left hemispheres of your brain which acts to balance your brain activity and mediate the particular areas of the brain which become over stimulated when we are angry.

Another brain balancing technique involves a specific type of movement of your eyes by first looking up as far as you can while keeping your face forward. Then you rotate your eyes clockwise, looking as far as you can in each direction until you have made a complete circle, first in one direction and then the other. You may need to repeat this a few times before feeling the calming effect, which will follow. Science has shown us that we have eye positions related to various emotional states and that by rotating them in this way; we are often able to reset our emotions back to a place of peace.

As you attempt to utilize these techniques, especially in the beginning, you will feel a reluctance to do them, or at least, do them with any real focus. This will be the result of the resistance mentioned earlier. When this resistance is felt, you will have come face to face with your greatest enemy on your path to choosing for yourself how you will react to what happens in your life, the part of you that wants you to stay just as you always have been and is struggling to maintain control over you.

If you have ever ridden a horse, you know that you have to be constantly vigilant and catch every attempt they make to run away with you at its very start. You do this because you know that once you have lost control and the horse has taken off in a full gallop there is little you can do to stop them.

It is exactly the same with our emotions. Being in your OO will allow you to begin catching yourself at the very start of a negative state so you don't lose control and let it run away with you. As you know, it is much easier to stop a negative state at its very beginning than later when it has become much more intense.

Normally someone finds themselves in a very negative place without seeing what led up to it and finds they are unable to stop it. This is why the process of constantly observing yourself from your OO is so important. It will give you the capacity to see what went unnoticed before, that is, each thing which occurred and altogether brought you to this intensely angry (or whatever) state.

Until we develop the capacity to see what leads us unknowingly toward these very dark places they will no doubt continue. Is there anything that can be done once the horse (your emotions) has run away with you? The answer is yes and no. Understand that no one can bring you out of this state other than yourself. So, only to the extent you are able to separate from it and become your OO, you will be able to alter that behavior. Once you have learned to do this, then the answer to the above question is yes, if you choose not to, then the answer will be no.

Perhaps in the beginning, even though you are trying to be in your OO you find yourself *seeing* that you are acting very angry, but are completely helpless to stop it. You may feel that this technique isn't working. However, the very act of finally seeing yourself reacting in this way is huge. It tells you that you have begun to change and over time as you continue practicing moving to your OO before, during and after these moments you will be able to gain more control over your emotions. All that is required is to continue this process every time you feel yourself beginning to slip. This behavior has run you for a very long time, be patient with yourself as you work to undo this strong conditioning.

You will begin to gain more and more control and there will eventually come a point where you truly see yourself as others do in those moments and this will cause you to feel very uncomfortable with what you see. This emotional discomfort will become stronger than the other emotion you have been attempting to control and will enable you to eventually let go of it entirely. *You will have changed;* you will have become more conscious of yourself and no longer be able to act unconsciously from your conditioning as before. This is the way you and everyone else changes, by becoming truly conscious of formerly unconscious behavior. Rather than seeing through the very limited tunnel vision caused by your conditioning, you will see your and the other person's behavior objectively and as a result come to feel very different in those moments. And those feelings will eventually make it impossible for you to act as you did before.

So far we have been discussing irritation and anger. What about anxiety and fear? The same exact techniques mentioned earlier can help in these cases as well. But there are others, for instance, when you are feeling anxious or fearful it can be very helpful to close your eyes and imagine yourself in someplace you feel safe and at peace. It can be a beach you've visited, a park you love, or any place where you felt completely safe and at peace. You can even make one up if you prefer.

It is important when you relax and visit this place, that you do it deeply. That is, feel the texture of the sand under feel, the water washing up over them as you walk along the shoreline. See the blue sky and clouds. Smell the ocean or the grass. Immerse yourself in the memory not just visually, but feel it, smell it, be there fully. And all the while you are doing this continue the tapping of either thigh as described earlier. Or alternately, you can wrap your arms around yourself, as if giving yourself a big hug, and alternately tap each shoulder.

These activities, letting go of any tension in your body, slowing down your breathing, visualizing yourself in some place you feel safe, eye rotation, and tapping alternately will bring you to a much more relaxed state. Reaching this place where you feel calm and peaceful may take a little time or happen quickly. However, one thing is for sure, the more you practice it, the faster your body will respond to this letting go of any tension, fear or anxiety.

If you are doing this at nighttime when you are laying in bed because you are having difficulty sleeping, you can add one final technique that will help you drift off to sleep. It works like this. Lie on your back with your legs extended in a natural, comfortable way and your arms along your sides.

Now focus on your toes and consciously relax them, and as you do this feel your feet beginning to become heavier. Now move to the balls of your feet and relax them, again feeling your feet becoming heavier. Next, move to your arches, then your heels, feeling them become completely relaxed and your feet still heavier. Continue this process with your ankles, calves, knees, thighs, hips, tummy, chest, lower back, upper back, shoulders, upper arms, lower arms, hands, fingers, and finally your neck, scalp and face. Do this slowly, and at each step as you relax an area, feel your entire body becoming heavier and sinking deeper and deeper into your bed.

It can be helpful to actually make a recording of you talking yourself through this process step by step very slowly (or download the one available from our website) and then listening to it at night when you are ready to go to sleep. It will also help if you create a routine where you prepare yourself for sleep by avoiding any stimulants a couple of hours before hand and making this pre-sleep period as calming as possible. Some people find a half hour of reading before getting ready to retire helpful. You will know what will work for you and as you create this routine and repeat it night after night your body will become accustomed to following it and you will find dropping off to sleep quickly becomes quite easy.

We have talked before about how trying to fix your conditioning while still in your conditioning is impossible. It is like trying to dry off while remaining in the pool. It just doesn't work. This is never more true than when someone finds themselves in a very bad place emotionally. An example of this would be someone who is feeling very frightened. It you try to have a conversation with them they will tell you how awful everything is. And anything they happen to think about during this time will add to their fear. Also, anything you say will be converted to something negative.

I call this 'being in the basement.' If you had a friend who happened to find themselves in the cold, dark basement of an abandoned house and they began to panic, everything they experienced while remaining in the basement would only increase their fear. Let's assume that you were upstairs in that same house and able to communicate with them.

They would be yelling "It is dark down here!" or "I am afraid." or "There are things down here that I can touch, and don't know what they are and they scare me!" Now you could tell them that it's not dark, or say to them; yes its dark, but that's ok, or you could tell them not be afraid, or that the things they felt were harmless. But it wouldn't help. No amount of dialogue would help *as long as they remained where they were.* The only thing that would help is for them to come up out of the basement, which would then result in their feeling better quickly.

This same thing occurs when someone is in a negative state. No conversation will help them as long as they remain in that dark place. Only by bringing themselves up to a higher place of consciousness, that is, letting go of that conditioned state, can they find relief.

111

The important thing to realize from what has been said is that when you or someone you know is in 'the basement,' any efforts to help whomever it is, must not be about what they are feeling down there (and will continue to feel as long as they are there regardless of what you say), *but rather about how to get them to a higher place.* Once this is achieved, they will be capable of being helped or finding their own answers to whatever was causing them to suffer.

You might try this the next time you encounter someone who is upset with you and venting. You could join them in the basement and argue back and forth which would only make things worse. Or, you could realize where they were and avoid any of their attempts to pull you down with them. You could say something like "I see that you are upset and would be happy to discuss this with you when you are feeling calmer."

No doubt, they would try even harder to pull you down where they are, but knowing what you now know would help you avoid being drawn into an argument by simply repeating again that you can see they are upset and will happily discuss whatever they feel the problem is when they are feeling calmer.

Later, when they had gotten to a better place, you might find that they had resolved the problem themselves. At the very least you would be able to have a rational conversation with them while you are in your OO and they were able to discuss whatever had upset them from a place of greater receptivity.

When someone's consciousness dips and they become angry, sad, depressed or whatever, their view of life becomes strongly affected by their emotional state and they are simply incapable of seeing reality clearly until they move out of that state.

Let's now take the example of someone feeling frightened or terribly inadequate. We know that having the normal types of conversation with them while they are in that place won't help. Listening to them explain why they are scared or feeling worthless will only reinforce their state. However, if you can help them to see that what they are feeling in the present (the fear or feeling of worthlessness) is something they were conditioned to feel when they were still quite young and unable to defend themselves, you will be helping to separate them from their conditioning. You can ask them if they remember times in their childhood when they felt this same way. They will answer yes. Next, you would ask them how many times they have felt this way throughout their lives. They won't be able to give you an exact number, but help them to realize this has happened many, many times. And that it will continue to happen countless times in the future.

Next help them understand that this extreme reaction was appropriate when they were little and unable to help themselves but has become their conditioned response to every similar situation that has happened to them since—even though they are no longer little and helpless. Ask them if they are more capable and stronger now than they were then. Help them to see that they are no longer a small child lacking the ability to defend themselves or see themselves more clearly, and that they can, now, as an adult change this conditioned response to whatever happened to bring them to this state.

If they are willing to discuss this with you and can begin to see that their response has nothing to do with the present, but is simply their conditioned response acting out, you will be helping them to become more conscious and separate from this negative state. It is important that you enable them to understand they have a choice and can begin to move away from all the useless suffering this conditioning would cause them in the future. Asking the right questions which caused them to stop and think moves them back to right brain functioning and away from their conditioning.

Not everyone is willing or able to give up their conditioning so there will be those who simply cannot yet be reached. But for those that are, these techniques can help immensely.

Another fact to consider is that, because of the conditioning someone received in their youth, they may, unconsciously of course, want to become upset, and experience that state and want you to be a player in their melodrama. You're trying to help them, by discussing at length what they are feeling, trying over and over again to help them, or arguing repeatedly with them could *simply be enabling their conditioning* to once again act out and give them what they need, not intellectually, but physiologically. From the perspective of your OO you may see this very clearly with people who are chronically unhappy, angry, or whatever.

Remembering that when you are activating your right brain, you are more conscious, gives us a way to help manage sadness and depression. You can't be in your conditioning, in this case depressed or sad, and pay strong attention to something else at the same time. Everyone has had the experience of being in a negative state when suddenly something happens which requires their focused attention. We do whatever it was that needed to be done that required all of our attention, and only afterwards realize that during that time our feeling of depression had disappeared.

This information tells us how we can move ourselves out of our sadness or depression. All we have to do is engage in an activity that requires our focused attention and consciously change our state. Solving a crossword puzzle works very well in these situations, as can any other activity, which requires your full attention. Experiment for yourself and find what activity you enjoy that requires your complete concentration and every time you begin to feel depressed engage in it. You will discover that the depression disappears and the more you do this, that is, reprogram yourself to not feel depressed, the less often the feeling returns. It can take time for you to rid yourself completely of this longtime conditioning, but if you do continue to do this exercise you will find the depression disappearing faster and returning less and then less frequently.

You will find additional techniques for getting out of the basement on our website www.dynamicnm.com.

Twelve - A Look Inside the Relationship of a Couple Experiencing The Quickening.

"Once in a while, right in the middle of an ordinary life, love gives us a fairy tale. Then the real challenge begins, can we keep from spoiling it with our small dark thoughts, our harsh judgments, or crush it beneath all of our emotional baggage?" ~ James LaFerla

We are now going to take a look at an individual who has been married twice. We will see how before, during and after her first marriage, she was completely helpless to do anything other than repeat the dysfunction she experienced in her youth. And then we will look at her second marriage and see how her ability to 'see' rather than 'be' her conditioning made it possible for her to have a very different experience.

You will find the contrast between her first marriage and her second rather dramatic. You will see how problems arise, as they do in all relationships, but because both individuals are capable of separating from their conditioning this allowed them to work through and eventually resolve their difficulties. Again, we will see the relationship through both her, and then his eyes respectively. These individuals too will share their most intimate feelings and tell us about the problems they encountered and how they were able to see them clearly, deal with them effectively, and get past them.

We will start with Linda. She is attractive, bright and has done very well in her work, rising to the position as Project Lead for a large financial organization. She says she is generally upbeat and happy. Her friends would also describe her as generally happy, strong willed, but very giving. Her present husband would strongly agree with those statements as well.

She is in her late 40's and has two daughters and a son from her previous and only other marriage. Her first marriage was very difficult for Linda. She says her husband was irresponsible, very cold, and either ignored her or treated her as if he was upset about something most of the time. He was also an alcoholic. They were not together long and after the separation she found herself a single mother with absolutely no support, financially or emotionally, from her ex-husband Don.

She tried getting back together with him a couple of times, but all the previous problems would just begin happening again. She spent most of her time after the separation working very hard to balance her demanding career with her role as a mother, quite often feeling very anxious about her ability to not only provide for her children, but somehow have the time and energy to be both father and mother to them.

Short history and an actual interview with Linda

She describes her mother as having a very strong personality and quite a bad temper. Their interactions consisted primarily of her mother being angry, criticizing her and making her feel worthless. Her only memories of her father were of his being drunk most of the time, also possessing a strong temper, constantly arguing with her mother, and almost never there. He left when she was quite young. Linda has three sisters and two brothers. She was the second oldest.

As she approached her teens, Linda remembers beginning to have even more difficulty getting along with her mother. She said she went through what she called a 'wild period' where it seem as if she was constantly doing just the opposite of what her mother demanded.

Question: Linda, can you tell us what it was about your first husband Don that caused you to fall in love with and then marry him?

Answer: I don't really know. He was a real loner and didn't seem to approve of or want anyone around him, including me. It certainly wasn't because he was good to me or even nice. The truth is, I didn't even like him that much, but for some reason I was drawn to him and even though I was very unhappy most of the time, I just couldn't seem to end it.

Question: So Linda, what happened?

Answer: Well, we dated for quite a while off and on. I went out with a couple of other men during this time who actually were quite nice to me, but always found myself drawn back to Don. So we continued to date and then eventually got married and moved in together.

Question: Was this a happy time for you?

Answer: No, I can't say that I ever really had happy times with Don. And after we moved in together, something very strange happened.

Question: What was that?

Answer: Well, before that time I pursued him pretty intensely and endured all of his, rejection, coldness and disapproval. But once we were living together, I suddenly felt very different toward him. It was as if I just didn't care about him anymore or what he thought of me. It was very odd. It was like we were there together, but it was as if I was living alone. We each had our own lives and didn't interact much. We basically stayed together out of convenience.

Question: So what finally brought you to the point where you decided to end the relationship?

Answer: By the last time we decided to give the relationship another try, we had a son and two daughters. Don tended to dote over the girls but pretty much treated our boy Dirk like he didn't care for him. The two of them never got along. Then one day Don came home in one of his usual bad moods and started in on Dirk, as he did so often. Dirk was just 13 at this time and Don, in the middle of his negative rant, took off his jacket and told Dirk to step outside, he was going to beat him up. I guess that was the final straw. I told Don to get out right then and never come back, and he did.

Linda's view of things

Linda believed that she was in love with Don even though he never treated her with anything remotely approaching love or consideration. And even though he never seemed very interested in her, she continued to pursue him. In her own words, "She just had to have him." Then after they began living together, she suddenly became ambivalent toward him, but never understood why. She says she continued to remain in this loveless, unhappy relationship off and on for years simply out of convenience, and was only able to finally end their relationship when Don threatened to physically attack their son.

For quite a few years after their final break up, Linda says she simply was never interested in having a relationship with another man. She spent most of her time working to support her children (receiving no financial help from Don) and every spare moment with her children.

Another view of her life from a higher level of consciousness

Now let's take a look at what really happened in Linda's first marriage. Let's see what Linda was unable to see for herself. As was the case with Kathy, you could have shared all of the information that follows with her, but it just wouldn't have registered, she would have been absolutely sure your assessment was wrong. *She's simply not capable of seeing her life objectively as a result of her present level of consciousness.*

What Linda was unable to see is that her original attraction for Don was simply her responding from her conditioning to his strong lack of interest, which felt like rejection to her. This was a pattern she learned with both her mother and father who were consistently emotionally unavailable. Don's disinterest in her compelled her to try (just as she had done as a child with her parents) to get him to love her. This irresistible attraction she had for him—what she called love—was simply her feeling the same desperate need she felt as a child, of trying to get love from someone unable to give it.

Because Linda received virtually nothing from Don emotionally, her children became the center of her universe. Her feelings of never having been loved or accepted by her mother drove her to overcompensate with her own children, denying them nothing. She consistently gave to them while receiving little in return. In time, they came to expect her to do whatever they wanted and would make her feel as if she was bad when she didn't.

They developed a strong sense of entitlement and (unconsciously of course) discovered that they could get their mother to do whatever they wanted simply by assuming the role of a disapproving parent and treating her like she was a bad child who could never live up to their expectations, regardless of how much she did for them. Her needs were unimportant to them and they showed her little in the way of consideration. She literally created the same situation she had with her mother with her own daughters, so she (her body) could re-experience all of the emotions she felt as a child.

Don rarely worked and so was able to spend much more time with the children. He was very affectionate with his daughters (adding to their sense of entitlement), but treated his son with either disregard or disapproval. Dirk, seeing the difference in how he was treated often felt unloved, sad, and grew increasingly angry. His father's treatment of him made him feel like an outcast in his own home, as though he was simply not deserving of the same love and consideration his sisters received so freely.

When he couldn't bear it anymore, he would turn to his mother who saw him as a victim of his father's neglect (much the way she felt in relation to the treatment from her own dad) and would attempt to make up for the love he was denied by his father by being overly caring and permissive. Dirk's awareness of his ability to receive this special consideration from his mother whenever he came to her feeling unloved, eventually began a pattern of his actually playing the victim whenever he wanted attention. It was his only way of evening out the field and receiving the love he needed.

In time, this role of playing 'poor me' became a habit (he literally came to see himself that way), of course, reinforced by his mother's extremely compassionate and loving reaction. As he grew older, it became more difficult to illicit the same loving response from her. And he responded by creating situations in his own life where he would be in need of help, often finding himself in trouble and eventually turned to drugs. Through it all, eventually his mother would respond by always 'being there' for him.

Linda never saw that she was compelled to seek out and marry someone very much like her father, and then recreated the presence of her mother through her treatment of her daughters. She didn't understand that she was turning them into people who would continue to feel this sense of entitlement with others and treat them with the same lack of consideration as they did her. Nor did she see how by showing her son too much love each time he came to her when he felt victimized that she was reinforcing behavior that would predispose her son to playing the helpless victim for the rest of his life and continually create situations where he needed help, to be rescued. Or how his constant rejection from his father would cause him to be drawn to the type of woman who would treat him in a similar way and he would find himself, as his mother did, stuck in a relationship trying to get love from someone unable to give it.

Linda was a single mother who lived much of her adult life as she did as a child, without any real love or consideration, in fact, just the opposite. Her conditioning as a child dictated what her life would be like forever. Her fate was sealed; she was condemned to spend the rest of her life unhappy. That is, had she not encountered this work and someone else who had been doing it for some time. We will see in her next relationship how those two factors changed everything.

A view of Linda's second marriage.

Question: Linda, can you tell us what it was about your second husband that caused you to fall in love and then marry him?

Answer: John was so different than anyone I had ever met. I felt a love from him that I had never experienced before in my life, a real love that was about me, not him. He introduced me to Dynamic Neuroplastic Mediation and many of its techniques. And we had these wonderful conversations where he was able to help me see my life from a different, more conscious perspective. This was something I had always wanted but never had. I knew there were things going on in my life that didn't feel right, I knew I wasn't happy, but from the perspective of my conditioning I was unable to see or do anything about any of this for myself.

Question: So Linda, what for you is different about this marriage than your first?

Answer: The biggest thing is how different John is from Don. We actually communicate with each other in a way I never have with anyone else. We are able to look at and examine our feelings from a place of real understanding. We don't fight, we problem solve from a place of mutual love and respect. As a result of our both working with DNM, and the ability it gave each of us to 'see' rather than 'be' our conditioning, we have developed an increasing capacity to separate from any conditioning that causes problems and instead allow us to move away from it.

Question: Can you tell us what sort of problems you've experienced in your second marriage?

Answer: Well, in the beginning, it was great. We hit it off immediately. It was as if we had known each other all of our lives. He was very good, not only to me, but to my two daughters which were still living at home during that time. The problems started when I began spending more and more time with John. My daughters had been used to having me there at their beck and call whenever they wanted and they began to make me feel as if I was deserting them even though I still spent almost every night at home, went to everyone of their sporting events, had just bought each of them a car, paid for all the groceries, and did all of the cooking and cleaning.

I should mention they were both about to enter college at that time, and after my first marriage, I never again had a relationship with anyone and devoted all of my spare time to my girls. I really thought when they finally saw me with someone who loved and cared about me and that I finally had a chance to have everything I had sacrificed all those years so I could take care of them that they would be happy for me, but it turned out they felt just the opposite. I was deeply hurt by their total lack of concern for my happiness if it in any way interfered with their own.

The work I was doing with DNM and John helped me see things about my relationship with my daughters that I had never noticed before. I saw how we have this ability to reconnect with our Original Observer and, as a result, see things less from our conditioning and much more objectively. It was after this that I began to become aware of things, like how one of my girls would demand that I take them shopping late at night after I had had a very long day at the office. They would let me pay for whatever they wanted and then simply walk out of the store, never saying "Thanks Mom." or even waiting for me.

John began going to all of the girl's softball games with me and we would always be discussing DNM, our conditioning, what we had noticed, etc. It was during this time that I was slowly starting to become more and more aware of aspects of my daughter's behavior that I had never noticed before.

For instance, after working very hard all day (my job is extremely demanding) I would drive out to whatever small town the games would be played, sit in on the bleachers in whatever weather and root them on. Then after the game was finished, I would go over to try to talk to them and they would rarely say more than one or two words to me before leaving with their friends. They did exactly the same thing on this particular day when John was standing with me. Afterwards, I discussed what I had noticed with him. He agreed that my observation was correct and we were able to discuss this in a way I never could have with anyone else before. Normally, had I not begun practicing being my OO and separating from my conditioning, I could not have been able to see their behavior objectively and if anyone tried to tell me about it, I would have become very upset. Without this change in my perspective, my relationship with John, had he said anything about their behavior, would have resulted in our relationship ending pretty quickly.

I was beginning to see more and more how inappropriate much of their behavior was and how I had raised my girls to be people who simply didn't have any empathy for anyone else, not even me. They never, for instance, said "Thanks" for coming to their games or ever once in all of their lives asked how my day was at work. Everything was always about them.

One night John stayed overnight at my place. The next morning he noticed that the girls would get up in the morning, walk right past me and not even saying good morning, it was as if I wasn't even there, or how they would leave without saying goodbye. I was amazed that I never noticed any of this behavior in 20 years of living with them! When you begin to see things from your Original Observer, you start to become aware of all sorts of things that you were simply unable to see before. As my capacity to separate from my conditioning increased and I was able to see my life and relationship with my daughters more objectively, I felt as if I had been walking around all of my life partially blindfolded.

John expressed how allowing this behavior was not only unfair to me, but to my girls as well, that this lack of consideration would cause them problems in any future relationships they had. I realized it was my job as the primary female figure in their lives to try to help them see this.

Question: So what did you do?

Answer: Well, I have to say, even though I saw this behavior, and was beginning to work on myself, it was still very difficult for me to say anything to them. But, I understood how important it was to help them see this behavior that would cause them so many problems in the future. So I sat down with them, and in the nicest way, shared with them how I felt. Then suddenly, I found myself confronted by both of them in a very emotional state saying they no longer knew who I was and that I was abandoning them.

Their response would hit me so hard emotionally in the beginning that I would find myself feeling as though what they were saying was the truth, and that I was somehow bad for wanting to actually have a life apart from them. As though, my needs for the love of a man and a relationship were simply my being selfish. Initially when this would happen, I would get completely lost in my conditioning, become very emotional and then pull away from John. I had not been working on myself for very long and simply wasn't able to resist being pulled deep down into those old patterns of behavior.

On more than one occasion after one of these confrontations with my daughters, I would tell John that I could no longer have a relationship with him. Had he not been working on himself as long as he had I doubt he could have dealt with all of that. After my first conversation with them about their behavior, they went from really liking John to seeing him in a very different light, even though he always continued to treat them with love and consideration and helped them whenever they needed it.

I was impressed by how he was able to return such negativity with love. It showed me what was possible by continuing this work. I am afraid that I was not handling things quite as well myself. I really was working very hard to try to see things from my Original Observer and lift myself out of my conditioning, but this situation would at times tear me apart.

Then, just when I thought things couldn't get any worse, I discovered that my sister, who had always been very competitive with me, was actually fueling those 'abandonment' fires. My daughters would go to her and tell her what I had said to them and she would agree with them that it was my problem, not theirs. She even went so far as to tell her friends and even mine that I was bad and deserting my girls.

When I first discovered what my sister was doing, my feelings were very hurt and I felt at times quite angry toward her. I no longer have those negative feelings because I understand now that she was just responding to her conditioned need to deal with her own extreme sense of inadequacy by placing me in a bad light. And how her need to receive more affection (really approval) from my daughters and the people, like those she told how bad I was, drove her to do these things. She was simply unconscious of her actions and couldn't see how much pain she was causing me or how her unwillingness to support me actually predisposed my daughters to more pain in their lives later on. Nor could my daughters see that rather than being helped, they were simply being enabled to continue their insensitivity toward others.

Question: So how did you and John get past all of this?

Answer: I will admit that it wasn't easy, but because of John's enormous patience and ability to discuss things with me without judgment or anger I began, slowly, to see the situation for what it was. I saw that I had transferred all of the feelings I would have normally had for a man in my life to my girls, and how I literally turned my daughters into my mother, being overly concerned with satisfying their every wish so they wouldn't stop loving me. By this time, they had become very used to that dynamic and knew exactly how to push my buttons. When I didn't do what they wanted they knew just how to make me feel like I felt when I lived with my mother, worthless and bad.

The feelings were so strong that, even though I saw them, it took me a while to be able to act against them. The strangest part is that I was actually compelled to continue enduring their lack of consideration, while I did everything for them, rather than being with John who treated me with great love and consideration. It's hard to believe how powerful the conditioning we receive as children is and how it can hold us in dysfunctional relationships no matter how unhappy we are.

Fortunately, for me, John had done a great deal of work on himself and was able to keep from falling into his own conditioning, and help me see my own.

Question: Have there been other problems?

Answer: Yes, there have. Because all of the relationships I had with men were with people who didn't treat me well, and then I went without a relationship for such a long time, I had sort of turned off my feelings toward men in general. I just never thought about them (ok, once in a while, if you know what I mean). But there had never been an equal giving and taking (I did all the giving), I just sort of lived in my own world and never thought about anyone other than my daughters. So when John and I were first together I continued thinking a great deal about my girls, but rarely considered him. Not ever having been in that type of relationship, where both people really care about and consider each other, I simply didn't know how to do it. And as a result, was very unfair with John.

Question: So how did you go about changing your behavior to make it possible for you to share in a truly loving relationship?

Answer: All I can say is thank goodness for DNM; we definitely never would have made it otherwise. I was steadily becoming stronger at becoming and remaining my Original Observer and not letting my conditioning take me over so completely. John was also very supportive during this time. Slowly, I became capable of talking to my girls without slipping into my conditioning. This helped immensely. I began more and more to see each situation from an objective point of view and as a result, my relationship with John continued to improve to where it is today. I am now able to live my life, mostly free (though I still have some work to do) from my conditioning and have a healthy, loving relationship with a man. Had I not been introduced to DNM and began working very hard to do it, I most certainly would have ended up just as my mother has, alone, unhappy, and never understanding why.

Question: What's happened with the girls?

Answer: They continue to resent John and tell others they don't like and even hate him and he continues to treat them consistently with love. I can see that they would have preferred things to stay the way they were, without me having anyone in my life but them. Sometimes I feel badly knowing that they have so little awareness of their behavior and have so little empathy or compassion for others. And as they are now, completely incapable of actually loving me.

At the same time, I know I created the situation, unconsciously, of course. But once I saw it, I wanted—no needed—to change it. I wanted to be happy. All I can do at this point is continue to love them from this more conscious place, in a more objective way, and hope that someday they will come around. I know that once they start having serious relationships with men they will encounter great difficulties because of their lack of awareness. I just plan to keep working on myself so when those times come, I can hopefully help them undo their previous conditioning and learn how to begin actually caring for others.

Another view of Linda's second marriage from a higher level of consciousness

Linda, like so many people, was essentially helpless to do anything to make her situation better because she was incapable of seeing the actual forces at work compelling her to repeat her childhood melodramas. Encountering this work and someone who had been doing it for some time allowed her to finally begin seeing things from a much more objective view. Seeing the real cause of her problems, she was then able to begin acting, rather than reacting, to her life in a way that allowed her to begin eliminating them.

In the beginning, because she was so new to this work, she had difficulty not being pulled down into her conditioning at times and as a result suffering. However, her intense desire to free herself from her dysfunctional patterns of behavior and constant work on herself allowed her to, more and more often, 'see' rather than 'be' her conditioning. She began moving away from being stuck with the life her childhood conditioning set her up for, to a very different life where she could experience real joy and happiness. It is no exaggeration to say that the quality of Linda's life from this point on will be dramatically better than it could have ever been otherwise. Unfortunately, many people never experience this freedom from their conditioning and are condemned to repeat it forever.

A view of another life from normal consciousness

This time our subject is John, Kathy's second husband. He is a successful computer programmer who owns his own business and has always been interested in anything having to do with self-improvement. He was always interested in Psychology, and became a Psych Major in college, turned to an in-depth study of Eastern philosophies and eventually discovered DNM.

He is athletic, outgoing and in his mid 50s. His friends would describe him as someone who is very easy going, intelligent, and quite kind. Linda says she would describe him exactly the same, with the addition that she has never seen him angry and is the most accepting, loving man she has ever known.

A short history and an actual interview with John

John says his family was pretty dysfunctional. His father had an incredibly bad temper and beat him often and nearly to death on more than one occasion. His mother possessed the same type of temper and struck him often as well. At the age of five, his mother left his father taking him with her. Within a few months she took John to the babysitter and never returned.

His grandmother and step grandfather came for him just as he was about to be put in a home. They took him back to live with them in a very small mining town in Idaho where they lived in abject poverty, moving constantly and often living in shacks without indoor plumbing. His step grandfather was an alcoholic who could never hold a job for more than a day or two and was constantly drunk.

At age nine, his mother returned for John. She had remarried and finally settled down. He was overjoyed to be with his mother again. However, this joy was short lived. Within days his mother began to beat and verbally abuse him again, constantly threatening to send him back to his Grandmother.

John's stepfather, who had grown up as a tough street kid didn't care much for him. He thought he was too sensitive and shy and couldn't understand why he didn't like watching football and other sports and thought he spent way too much time alone reading.

At twelve, John's stepfather died and his mother was barely able to provide for them. They moved to the inner city and John began shining shoes every night after school until the bars closed so he would have money for food and clothing. His mother was rarely home, spending most of her time with one man or another.

At the age of fifteen, they moved again, this time to a nicer neighborhood. This is where he met and fell deeply in love with a beautiful young classmate. They saw each other practically every day for most of the next year. John was extremely happy during this time and expected to remain that way. Fate had other plans.

One Saturday after taking his girlfriend to do some shopping they got back in John's car. Suddenly she gasped for air and slumped over in the seat unconscious. He raced to the gas station across the street and called 911. It was too late. She was dead from an illness that caused her body to create blood clots; one which had became logged in her heart and ended her life as John held her in his arms waiting for the ambulance. John never returned to school and moved away from home within a few weeks of his girlfriend's death

Question: John, can you tell us what it was about Linda that caused you to fall in love and then marry her?

Answer: I knew from the first time I spoke with Linda that she was special. She was obviously very smart, and like me, loved to learn anything new. She had a great sense of humor and was not afraid to share her true feelings with me. I guess the main thing though, was that I could tell that she was someone who cared deeply about others and had a real hunger to increase her understanding of herself and people in general. When I told her about DNM, she said it was exactly what she had been looking for to help her understand her life better and jumped in with both feet.

Question: What sort of problems did the two of you encounter as the relationship developed?

Answer: Well, after we started spending more time together, her daughters would call her and really treat her pretty rough for not being with them whenever they wanted her there. I could see that those phone calls would really hurt her.

Question: So what did you do?

Answer: Linda and I had lots of conversations about her childhood, her previous marriage and her children. She was not afraid to be very open and honest about her life. We also talked a lot about this work and I explained the techniques of DNM to her, such as, how seeing from her Original Observer would help her increase her awareness of everything that was happening, and to see it more objectively. I understood how she had, in the past sought out relationships like those she had as a child. We discussed all of this and also how she had actually turned her girls into her mother and reacted to them exactly as she had to her.

Question: Did that help?

Answer: Yes it did. I mean she really got it intellectually. Like I said, she is very bright. Unfortunately, her conditioning related to these issues was incredibly strong and she would find herself being pulled back into those feelings of being a worthless child frequently. Her daughters are absolute masters at manipulating her emotionally and knew just which buttons to push.

But to Linda's credit, even in the beginning, she was willing to work against her conditioning and even tried to have conversations with them and share her feelings. This took a great deal of strength. Here she was trying to make a major change in her way of relating to her girls and everyone was resisting her with all their might, I mean they were really hard on her.

Question: Did things get worse or better?

Answer: Anytime someone attempts to change their conditioning there are going to be moments when they take one-step forward and then two steps back. It is a natural part of the change process; you can't just snap your fingers and change a lifetime of conditioning. So I would have to say both, at times better and at other times worse. But never for a moment did I doubt Linda's commitment to changing her life. I knew it would get rough at times, and I also knew she needed time. I didn't push or pull at her emotionally, I just let her work through it at her own pace, all the while attempting to be consistently supportive.

Question: How did you feel when Linda would pull away from you emotionally and even tell you she didn't want to have a relationship with you any longer? How did you deal with that?

Answer: By remaining in my Original Observer and not allowing my conditioning to come in to play. Because of this work, one of the things I have come to see is that we are all a study in opposites. We sometimes swing to one extreme and at other times go to the other. I knew that her reaction—telling me that she didn't want to have a relationship with me—was her swinging way over to one side. I also knew she wouldn't stay there. I understood that if I allowed myself to slip into my conditioning and become negative with her (give her more of what she was already getting from everyone else) that it would only make things worse.

134

Question: Wasn't it difficult?

Answer: I can't say that it was always easy, but after you have been doing this work for a while, separating from your conditioning becomes much easier. Also, the more you do it, the more you see how allowing yourself to go with your conditioning never makes things better and just creates more suffering for you and most likely those around you. When you truly see how going with your conditioning causes you to lose yourself and your ability to be objective or even love another person, you really, really don't want to go there.

Question: So what happened next?

Answer: I saw how hard Linda fought to mediate the swinging back and forth from her conditioning to her Original Observer and how incredibly brave she was through that struggle with those unbelievably powerful emotions that constantly wanted to control her. She continued to slip back from time to time into her conditioning, but with less and less frequency. She became stronger and stronger and I knew, in time, she—and we—would be fine. And that's exactly how it has worked out. All of this actually brought us closer together and gave us a deeper understand of, and appreciation for each other.

John's view of things

John says he saw Linda's intense desire to change her life and how hard she was working to do just that. He says he believed in her ability to work through their problems, given enough time and support. He believed by not descending into his conditioning and reacting with anger and just allowing Linda the time she needed to become stronger she would be fine.

Another view of his life from a higher level of consciousness

We can see how John was actually acting from a higher level of consciousness. And so, instead of breaking off the relationship or getting angry and making things even more difficult for Linda, he was able to provide the true love and support she needed to figure things out for herself.

We chose this specific couple for a reason. We wanted to illustrate how someone, even with all of the intense trauma John had experienced during his childhood, could eventually free himself of it. And beyond that, while having to 'see' rather than 'be' his conditioning, with Linda pushing all of his buttons, he was able to help her 'see' and as a result begin to free herself from her conditioning as well.

Had John not been working on himself as he had, his childhood conditioning would have dictated his responses to what happened and the results would have been very different. In a previous interview, he shared with us how far less capable he had been in dealing with problems that occurred in his relationships when he was younger and before beginning this work.

He confirmed what we could predict from hearing of his childhood experiences, that John developed the natural tendency to become extremely angry or at other times, very anxious (as a result of the beatings he received from both his mother and father). And also how, being left by his mother resulted in still more anger, feelings of worthlessness and a hypersensitivity to anything that felt like abandonment. He told us how he eventually came to understand how his feeling worthless caused him to become hypersensitive to criticism and compelled him to become an overachiever, constantly trying to prove to himself and the rest of the world that it wasn't true.

The ultimate success they had in working past their problems was because they each understood that only working from a higher place of consciousness, their Original Observer would allow them to make progress. They realized that anything they did from their conditioning would only make matters worse.

Unfortunately, most people react from their conditioning in these types of situations and that is why there are so many failed marriages and relationships. We have seen how this doesn't have to be the case. How anyone who really wants to have a happy relationship can do so by modeling the behavior of Linda and John. Fortunately, the Quickening is making this even more possible.

Thirteen - Getting Back to Center.

"The best and safest thing is to keep u bulance in your life, acknowledge the great powers around us and in us. If you can do that, and live that way, you are really a wise man." ~ Euripides

Earlier I discussed how we develop what I call disparate extremes, personalities that are polar opposites of each other in our youth and how we are unconsciously driven by them our entire life. I will give you a personal example of how this happened in my life. When I was a child, my family was exceedingly poor. Ever piece of clothing I wore came from a rummage sale, was usually in bad shape, outdated, and almost never fit me properly. I was keenly aware that I looked different than most of the other kids and was, at times, teased because of my odd attire. I almost always felt embarrassed about my appearance and my sense of self worth suffered as a result.

My parents were both very angry most of the time and fought with each other frequently. When they were not hurling insults (or objects) at each other, they would turn to me. I was told repeatedly and with great intensity how worthless I was, how they wished they had never had me, and that I would never amount to anything, etc. The rest of the time, they mostly ignored me.

The consistent message I received growing up was that I was worthless. I internalized that concept and came to see myself as poor, not very bright, certainly not worth loving and somehow defective. The pendulum had swung from my being capable of having an objective view of myself (being my OO) to an extreme where I could only see myself as inferior to everyone around me that seemed to have more—deserve more—than I, including parents who loved and accepted them.

This view of myself kept me from ever trying to do well in school. I accepted this negative picture of myself as the truth. I always passed each grade, but just barely and saw no reason to study or try to do any better. Why should I? What would be the point?

Then at the age of 16, I encountered an extraordinary man, the first really good teacher I had ever had. He saw see me as someone who was capable of achieving more and was determined to help me share his view. He made sure, if he asked me a question that I would know the answer. And when I did answer correctly, he would provide lots of positive reinforcement. Suddenly, I found myself needing to show him that I could do well and began studying very hard. It was the first time in my life I received an 'A' in any class.

This man's loving approach to teaching woke something up in me and I became so excited to see that I could do well that I began getting straight 'A's in every class. From this point on in my life, I became an overachiever in everything I did. My apathy toward learning and any form of competition, resulting from my low self-image, was replaced by an incredible drive toward excellence. *The pendulum had swung from one extreme to the other.* I had become the mirror opposite of my conditioned self. Because I had always felt so terribly inadequate up to this point, the desire to win or achieve and prove it wasn't true became the driving force in my life.

In college, I maintained a 4.0 average. I learned to dance and became the Dance Director for the Fred Astaire Dance Studios. I competed in full contact Karate and won every match. I had become extremely competitive. Being the best became a way for me to prove to others, but mostly myself, that I was neither stupid nor worthless. By the time I was twenty-two I started my first business, which did very well and allowed me to purchase an expensive new car and a rather nice assortment of suits. What's important to see here is not what I did, but *why* I was doing it. I was not the one in charge of my life, my conditioning was deciding, driving me to constantly overachieve.

My life continued this way well into my 40s. I kept making more and more money, and competing in everything from English riding and jumping to chess. But I was starting to see that no amount of money, or success in competition would ever change the quality of my inner life. I had reached what others might see as the pinnacle of success and yet, rather than becoming happier, I was actually growing increasingly dissatisfied with my life.

The pendulum had swung completely to the other side. I was thought of as very bright and capable, wore very expensive clothes, drove a new Mercedes 500 SL, ate at the finest restaurants, dated lots of women, and still something was missing...I wasn't really happy. How could this be? I had always believed that if I became successful enough that I would find true happiness. I could see very clearly now that this assumption was wrong and became absolutely determined to find out what I needed to do to finally reach this elusive state of inner peace.

In an effort to try to understand myself and others better I had started reading psychology books at age 12 and eventually became a Psychology major in college. When I had read virtually everything available on the subject without finding the answers I was looking for I turned to Eastern Philosophy, Neurobiology, Hypnotism, NLP, Quantum Physics, Acupuncture, EMDR, Applied Kinesiology, Bioelectromagnetic Medicine, an in-depth study of the physiology of the brain and body, and anything else I could find that might help me understand myself and others better. This search continued intensely throughout my life and ultimately resulted in my having an experience, which dramatically changed my consciousness forever and allowed me to finally see what was wrong with my life and how to change it.

I could see that I wasn't living consciously, but rather like some sort of robot incapable of doing anything but responding to its programming. Programming which had occurred during my childhood. I saw that I was compelled to swing to the other extreme in a constant effort to prove to myself I wasn't worthless and stupid. Everything I had accomplished so far—my entire life— was simply me *unconsciously* overcompensating for a sense of inferiority. My conditioning was running my life, not me.

Now seeing my life objectively and no longer wanting to remain trapped in it, I decided to give away my business and most of the money I had. Then I put what little I could pack in my car, and left everything behind without any idea of where I would go or what I would do. All that was important to me at this point was no longer being what I had become; I needed to create a new life, which would allow me to find and live in harmony with my true self.

I am not recommending such a radical change to anyone, but it was exactly what I needed. For the next few years, I lived on the edge of poverty and mostly in solitude. I experienced very dark moments when I was sure I had made an awful mistake and was very tempted to return to my former life. The pain I experienced at these times was indescribable. Fortunately, there were other periods where I was taken over by an incredible sense of peace. The person I had been before—my conditioning—was dying and I felt, and was frequently overwhelmed, by a terrible sense of dread accompanied by an intense feeling of hopelessness and worthlessness that, was it not for the Quickening, would have been more than I could bear.

However, over time, I was able to see more and more of the conditioning, which was responsible for all of my suffering and let it go. The more this happened, the more at peace I became. I eventually found my true self and no longer needed to prove anything to anyone, especially myself. At last, I was no longer driven by my conditioning to be this or that. And as I let go of any judgment about myself, I became capable of doing the same with others. I was able to just be and experienced a peace I had never before known. Along with this peace came a tremendous feeling of compassion for others and ability to accept everyone just as they are. It was no longer necessary for me to try to change who I was in an attempt to receive love from others and no one had to change or do anything other than be who they were to receive mine.

The experience which altered my consciousness combined with this intense period of inner work allowed me to become free of my conditioning and to see what I could never have seen otherwise. For instance, from this place of higher consciousness, I became aware that there are three phases which may occur in every individual's life. The first happens with the conditioning we receive as a child, which causes us to move away from an objective view of ourselves to some extreme as I had. The second phase begins as we attempt to somehow compensate for whatever insufficiency or insufficiencies we then believe we have. Driven unconsciously for the remainder of our life, with our conditioning deciding for us how we will work, handle relationships and essentially every other aspect of our behavior. Some overcompensate, like I did, others simply give up and accept this negative view of themselves, becoming trapped in this false sense of themselves.

The third phase, which almost never occurs, happens when someone begins to see the extent to which they are driven by their early conditioning and begin letting go of it so the pendulum no longer swings to one extreme or the other, but returns finally to the center. It is only in this middle place where one can begin to get in touch with their real self and start living their life *free to be who they really are.* This third phase is where, those who are able to attain it, find real peace and happiness.

People getting stuck at phase two can be seen everywhere you look; the workaholic husband who pushes himself too hard, frequently feeling extreme stress, sacrificing time with his wife and or family. He believes this is just who he is, never realizing that he is simply overcompensating for a sense of inadequacy and so lives a life very different from what it could be.

I have known many women trapped in this same situation where doing a good job is never enough. They must do more and still more just to avoid feeling inadequate. At the other extreme, we see people who simply drop out of the race, accepting that they will never be any good and often turn to drugs or alcohol to escape those negative feelings.

The examples are endless, mothers and or fathers who are too strict with their children or become too permissive. Men who must have one woman after another, possibly cheating on their wives because they need the positive reinforcement the next conquest brings. Of course, there are women who attempt to feel better about themselves and do the same.

Then we have people who become too controlling in an attempt to make sure their life and everyone in it does what they need them to do. And their opposites who simply give up because they feel there is no use trying. We can add to this list those whose underlying fear causes them to be too angry with others and act in ways that undermine their relationships and create the very thing they are afraid of.

Hopefully what you can see from all of this is that we all normally get trapped in phase two and are never able to free ourselves, living our entire lives trying to overcome the feelings we were conditioned to have as a child, and most importantly...*that this will never lead us to real peace and happiness in our lives.*

This is where we must ask ourselves the most important of questions, "Who would we be without our conditioning?" That is, find out, not *how* we are, but *who* we really are. When you, through using your OO to observe yourself, begin to drop your conditioning, you will become ever more capable of seeing your true self.

There is a quote from Michael Angelo after being asked how he carved such beautiful statues from big chunks of blank stone where he answered, *"I just chip away what doesn't belong there."* And so it will be with us, and as we chip away more and more of our conditioned self, our true self will slowly emerge. Once this connection with the essential you occurs and you begin to live in harmony with that, the quality of your life will change dramatically.

Many people, at some point in their life become aware that they are not living the life they want, leading some to have what is called a 'Mid Life Crisis.' They know something is wrong and desperately want to change their life to finally be happy. However, because they normally don't understand the true dynamics of their situation, their choice of solutions provides no help. This can be seen with middle-aged men who suddenly buy a sports car or motorcycle and begin acting as if they were in their 20's again, or the couple who sells everything and moves to some remote location out in nature, only to find they are still unhappy. The old adage *"Where ever you go, there you are."* applies here. Their problem is not where they are, but rather what they have become and their inability to see that this conditioning will follow them wherever they go.

I could have become more and more wealthy for the rest of my life and never found happiness. It was only by seeing that I was being driven by my deep seated sense of inadequacy and coming to grips with that, and then becoming aware of any other negative conditioning and eliminating it which finally brought me peace.

Learning to rid myself of the conditioning, which made me feel the need to overachieve, judge myself too harshly, become frustrated and at times angry, finally allowed me to experience a level of happiness no amount of success could have ever brought. The only way out, the only solution is to use your OO to come to see what you are, and then, through a process of elimination, find out who you really are. Find the extremes in yourself. See what's driving you to continue the life you have now and having the same life experiences. As you change that, real peace and happiness will quickly follow.

Fourteen - Generally Accepted "Myths" and Their Effects On Our Consciousness.

"When your mind is liberated your heart floods with compassion: compassion for yourself, for having undergone countless sufferings because you were not yet able to relieve yourself of false views, hatred, ignorance, and anger; and compassion for others because they do not yet see and so are imprisoned by false views, hatred, and ignorance and continue to create suffering for themselves and for others." ~ Thich Nhat Hanh

There are a number of generally accepted 'truths' which every population seems to adopt automatically. These are simply taken to be the truth because when we are exposed to them growing up, everyone else seems to accept them as facts. For instance, if you had grown up a few hundred years ago, and someone asked you if the world was flat or round, you would have been like "Duh, of course it's flat." Whole generations of people went through their entire lives believing this untruth and never questioned it for a moment. It made perfect sense to them. Why question it? And if you had told them the earth was really a round ball spinning in space, they would have thought you were crazy. There have always been generally accepted 'truths' like this. The problem is that when you are raised in a society where everyone believes something—even when it's not the truth—it's hard not to, without ever really thinking about it, incorporate this 'truth' into your own belief system. That is, believe in and have your thinking affected by something that is simply not true.

These generally accepted notions, or what I refer to as myths, can have a profound influence on the way we view ourselves and others. In our previous example (of the earth being flat) explorers of that time were convinced if they ventured too far they would simply fall off into oblivion. This fear of impending doom awaiting anyone reckless enough to go beyond areas already known had a serious impact on our world; dramatically limiting the discovery of other parts of the world, cultures, products, trade, and the economy of nations. Every period in time has its myths and those who believe them. This chapter is to help whoever wishes to see, at present, some of our society's myths for what they really are and as a result begin to become free from their negative influence.

Myth #1 - The idea that everyone is perfectly capable of Changing their behavior and always doing the 'right' thing, if they really want to.

"At this level, the individual perceives the maintenance of the expectations of his family, group, or nation as valuable in its own right, regardless of immediate and obvious consequences."
~ Lawrence Kohlberg

This idea that everyone is perfectly capable of changing their behavior and always doing the 'right' thing, if they really want to, that is, if they are not emotionally defective, weak, a 'bad' person, or simply insane, turns us all into hypocrites. We are told not to lie, and yet everyone does at times. We find this middle place where we feel it's actually ok to lie when we believe it's necessary and still think of ourselves as essentially honest. Teenagers are told they shouldn't think about—and certainly not have—sex, at a time when their body chemistry is compelling them to do just the opposite. We are told to put others before ourselves, but often find it impossible to do. We are supposed to be the perfect parents who love our children and consistently do exactly the right thing for them, but of course, that's impossible as well. And in the end, we muddle through all of this, doing the best we can, and rationalize any behavior that seems less than ideal. Uncomfortable with our own inability to live up the unrealistic standard society has set for us, we often blame our shortcomings on others, e.g. "I know I shouldn't get so mad at her, but who wouldn't when she does...(this, that or whatever).

This Myth, this model of perfection we are expected to live up to, and the idea that we should be able to control our behavior with our minds—by others who can't do it either—and which has simply not been possible, creates enormous stress and is in part responsible for the tremendous rise in the use of antidepressants and anti-anxiety drugs, not to mention the so called recreational drugs and alcohol.

Until now, with The Quickening, and the tools for change which are becoming available because of it, such as those provided by DNM, we simply haven't been able to free ourselves from certain types of behavior or reach anything near our true potential. Still, we all grew up subject to societies unrealistic expectations of how we should behave. Yet, every statistic on divorce, family trauma, suicide, and violence tells us something is terribly wrong with our present paradigm, it just isn't working. The actual truth is that everyone, no matter how dysfunctional their life, is doing the best they can with the tools and help (if any) they have been given.

The more someone has strongly adopted this myth into their psyche the more difficult it will be to accept what I have just said. They will continue to judge themselves, and of course, others harshly. They will see people who are overweight as being weaklings, those who don't make a good income as lazy, those who aren't capable of having a happy relationship as emotionally immature, and the list could go on forever. Never mind that they themselves may not be in that good of shape, make as much money as they think they should, and don't have a happy relationship either. Let me say it again, **with the conditioning they experienced, and the tools and help each person has received (including you and I)...everyone is doing the best they possibly can.**

Recalling the situation that occurs with almost everyone with varying intensity at times, where they are experiencing an implicit memory, we now know that their response is something they have very little or no control over. The idea that anyone who has this type of reaction should be able to just change it with their mind simply shows a gross lack of insight into the way our emotions work and the tremendous power they have to control us.

Should someone who has claustrophobia be thought of as bad when they react strongly to a situation which causes them fear? Should we become angry at them for their response? How about the war veteran who becomes extremely anxious as a helicopter passes overhead or some other incident triggers his implicit memory? Are their responses really any different than someone else who responds to the extreme conditioning they received growing up? Hopefully, you realize the answer is no. And also that whomever this is happening to should be seen as someone who is unable to do any better at that moment, someone who needs help, someone who is suffering and deserves not our harsh judgment and anger, but rather compassion.

When someone fails to live up to society's expectations they are generally judged as 'bad.' You know for yourself that there have been times in your own life when you were going through a difficult time and acted in a way you wish you hadn't. You also know that at those moments you were probably judged by others as being 'bad.' Were you really bad, or simply someone doing the best you could under those particular circumstances? If we were to examine closely anyone's life who judged you to be 'bad' we could—without exception—find examples in their life where others thought of them as bad, perhaps even worse than you.

So the net result of all of this judging ourselves and others results in even more hypocrisy. Someone pulls out in front of you and you consider them a jerk. You have at one time or another done something similar and had others think the same of you. None of us are perfect and never will be. We will all continue to do things we regret at times. What you, and everyone else, needs at those moments is compassion, not reflexive, conditioned judgment and anger. We can just see it happening and realize that people will do things we might not like at times, just as we sometimes do things others may find objectionable. It is just how we—every single one of us—are at times. By remembering that we ourselves are fallible, we can just let whatever is happening happen and give them the same consideration we would like to receive the next time we make a mistake. Whenever I find myself in a situation where someone is doing something that could be considered rude, I simply say to myself "That's how we are at times." Truly understanding that this really is how we all are at times puts the situation in proper perspective and allows us to not react negatively.

As long as we, without realizing it, believe that we should live up to this extreme model of perfection and judge ourselves harshly, we will do the same to others. Allowing ourselves to see that we aren't and don't have to be perfect, that we are doing the best we can will allow us to have more empathy for others when we see someone acting in a way that is less than perfect.

Wouldn't it be nice if the next time you got angry, irritated, or did something that could be perceived as 'bad,' the other person, or persons, involved reacted, not from their conditioning with judgment, anger or resentment, but rather from a more conscious place with compassion? And what if you began to make a habit of doing the same for the next person who cuts you off in traffic or says something you find insensitive?

When we begin to see people from this new perspective—that they are doing the best they can—our reaction to them will begin to change from a typical negative conditioned response, which results in our suffering and very likely the other person as well, to something quite different. Our empathetic and compassionate response will begin to change those people at their very core level, even if you cannot see it happening at that moment.

Understanding that sometimes we all act badly, will allow you to not take others behavior personally and avoid reacting from your conditioning. As you begin to do this, you will find that your day becomes more and more filled with peace. And know that every conscious act of kindness has a rippling effect and each time you do this you are affecting others much more than you know, drawing them toward the same behavior, and making the world a better place.

Myth #2 - Children of dysfunctional families are seen as victims only up to a certain age, then suddenly they are no longer victims, but instead seen as 'bad.'

"Children exposed to violence experience considerable short-and long-term harm. This includes experiencing feelings of helplessness, hopelessness, fear, and aggression when their parents, loved ones, or they themselves are harmed. Long-term effects include difficulties in school, work, and relationships and physical and mental health problems. In addition, children exposed to violence may be victimized again as they grow older."
~ U.S. Department of Justice

Seeing children who were treated badly as victims only up to a certain age and then suddenly seeing them as bad shows the degree to which our society is capable of being unconscious and as a result terribly unjust. The truth is that we all grow up in families that are dysfunctional to some degree. And, with rare exceptions, most of us remain victims of that conditioning, be it more or less severe, throughout the rest of our lives. The baggage we accumulated as children doesn't suddenly disappear on our 16th or 21st birthday.

If you really understood how false Myth #1 is you can see the problem here. These children who were mistreated in their youth will continue to be affected by it as adults. However, just because they have gotten a little older they are suddenly seen in a very different way. Like the rest of us, they do the best they can to resist their conditioning, but with the tools and help they have been given, they are simply not able to free themselves from all they experienced as a child.

A woman who grew up with a mother who was overly controlling will very likely be the same with her children, or flip and go to the other extreme becoming instead overly permissive. So as much as she may love her children, she is going to be compelled to be overly controlling which will then affect their lives in a negative way, or be too permissive and affect their lives in a different, but still negative way. Shouldn't she simply be able to be the perfect mother despite her own conditioning? The answer is a resounding NO. She is simply doing the best she can, having been programmed the way she was. She is still a victim, just as she was as a child, someone who needs help seeing her conditioning and the tools to begin changing it. Hopefully, this will begin to change your idea of their being 'bad' people out there who need to be punished.

There would no doubt be some who would say that she is a 'bad' mother because she is way too hard on her children, or that she just lets them run wild and get into all sorts of trouble. Is she a 'bad' mother? Should she be judged like that? If you believe so, you are still not seeing the truth of the human condition. You can't be brought up in a dysfunctional world by dysfunctional parents and not wind up dysfunctional to some degree yourself. You can pretend that you can, or actually believe it, but it is simply not the truth.

Another example would be that of a boy who was beaten severely by his parents growing up. He too would be seen as a victim up to a certain age. And again, because he never received the help or the tools to free himself from his conditioning, he is very likely to become a battering parent. What's important to understand is that *he is still a victim of his conditioning,* not someone that needs to be punished (given more of what he received as a child), but instead the help to see his conditioning and the tools to begin changing it. Is some sort of intervention called for, absolutely, so his child does not perpetuate this battering cycle.

But there is a tremendous difference between seeing this man, who was a victim of a battering parent as still a victim, verses simply seeing him as someone who is 'bad.' The first view will be one of compassion and result in his beginning to get the help he needs to free himself from the behavior so that finally, he may have a chance for happiness. The second view simply sees him as someone who should be punished.

It is essential to really grasp the inhumanity of treating someone who had a difficult or even terrible childhood once they reach adulthood as 'bad' and then punishing them still more! They didn't have anything to say about the conditioning they were receiving. The last thing they would have wanted, if they truly had a choice, would be to grow up and act like the person who brutalized them as an infant. They suffer severely and need help, not yet more pain in their lives.

Myth #3 - You are who you are, and you as well as others need to learn to just accept that.

"Life is a process of becoming, a combination of states we have to go through. Where people fail is that they wish to elect a state and remain in it. This is a kind of death." ~ Anais Nin

This myth that we are who we are and should just accept it and expect everyone else to do the same, and that somehow through this acceptance, you will find peace and happiness couldn't be further from the truth. The previous chapters have shown you how we can, in fact, change our behavior and have given you some DMN strategies to begin doing just that. Saying that you are who you are and accepting it, certainly makes us feel good, but it eliminates any possibility for you to evolve personally. If you have a problem with anger, do nothing to change this, and expect others to just accept it, you will never find peace or happiness. The only way is by using your OO to discover for yourself who you really are, beginning to see your conditioned behavior that creates problems in your life or holds you back from reaching your true potential and begin changing it.

Myth #4 - Most of the people we see everyday are, in general, doing fine.

"What do we live for if not to make life less difficult for each other?" ~ George Eliot

Our mistaken perception that most of the people we see everyday are doing fine, stems from the fact that most people are acting as if that were the truth. As discussed earlier there is a great deal of pressure on each of us to live up to societies ideal that we should all be successful in our work, our relationships, and every other aspect of our lives. We all attempt to maintain this facade, even when our life situation is far from ideal, which is usually the case.

This false idea that everyone else is fine keeps us from having as much compassion for others as we might if we really understood what their life is really like. The truth is that many of us are having a very difficult time trying to reach that ideal and suffer much more than anyone suspects.

If you doubt this, consider the following statistics from The World Health Organization (WHO), the American Institute on Domestic Violence, www.gdcada.org, and research done by Bob Murray, PhD and Alicia Fortinberry, MS:

* The health-related costs of rape, physical assault, stalking, and homicide by intimate partners exceeds $5.8 billion each year.
* 85-95% of all domestic violence victims are female.
* 5.3 million Women are abused each year.
* 1,232 women are killed each year by an intimate partner.
* Women are more likely to be attacked by someone they know rather than by a stranger.
* Homicide is the leading cause of death for women in the workplace.
* Each week, child protective services (CPS) agencies throughout the United States receive more than 50,000 reports of suspected child abuse or neglect. In 2002, 2.6 million reports concerning the welfare of approximately 4.5 million children were made. In approximately two-thirds (67 percent) of these cases, the information provided in the report was sufficient to prompt an assessment or investigation. As a result of these investigations, approximately 896,000 children were found to have been victims of abuse or neglect—*and average of more than 2,450 children per day.*
* *Since 1964, the U.S. crime rate has increased by as much as 350%,* and over 11 million crimes were reported in the year 2007 alone.

* Depressive disorders affect approximately 18.8 million American adults or about 9.5% of the U.S. population age 18 and older in a given year.
* Everyone will at some time in their life be affected by depression—their own or someone else's.
* Preschoolers are the fastest-growing market for antidepressants. At least four percent of preschoolers—over a million—are clinically depressed.
* *The rate of increase of depression among children is an astounding 23%.*
* 30% of women are depressed. Men's figures were previously thought to be half that of women, but new estimates are suggest they are higher.
* 54% of people believe depression is a personal weakness.
* 41% of depressed women are too embarrassed to seek help.
* 80% of depressed people are not currently receiving any treatment.
* 92% of depressed African-American males do not seek treatment.
* *Depression will be the second largest killer after heart disease by 2020*—and studies show depression is a contributory factor to fatal coronary disease.
* Depression results in more absenteeism than almost any other physical disorder and costs employers more than $51 billion per year in absenteeism and lost productivity, not including high medical and pharmaceutical bills.
* More than 100,000 U.S. deaths are caused by excessive alcohol consumption each year.
* At least once a year, the guidelines for low risk drinking are exceeded by an estimated 74% of male drinkers and 72% of female drinkers aged 21 and older.
* Nearly 14 million Americans meet diagnostic criteria for alcohol use disorders.
* More than 18% of Americans experience alcohol abuse or alcohol dependence at some time in their lives.

* Traffic crashes are the greatest single cause of death for person aged 6-33. About 45% of these fatalities are in alcohol related crashes.
* Alcohol kills 6.5 times more youth than all other illicit drugs combined.
* 50% of high school seniors report drinking within the last 30 days, with 32% report being drunk at least once.
* About 22.5 million Americans aged 12 or older in 2004 were classified with past year substance dependence or drug abuse.
* 1 in every 4 people, or 25% percent of individuals, develops one or more mental disorders at some stage in life. Today, 450 million people globally suffer from mental disorders in both developed and developing countries. Of these, 154 million suffer from depression, 25 million from schizophrenia, 91 million from alcohol use disorder and 15 million-drug use disorder.
* Mental illnesses are more common than cancer, diabetes, or heart disease.
* As many as two-thirds of all people with a diagnosable mental disorder do not seek treatment, whether for fear of being stigmatized, fear that the treatment may be worse than the illness itself, or lack of awareness, access and affordability of care.
* Mental illnesses rank first among illnesses that cause disability in the United States, Canada, and Western Europe.
* Many people suffer from more than one mental disorder at a given time.
* Mental illness is a serious public health challenge that is under-recognized as a public burden.

The toll of mental illness is tragic: *Suicide claims a life every 16 minutes. Think of that...every 16 minutes someone reaches a point where they would rather die than continue to endure their life!*

According to the American Foundation for Suicide Prevention: *"It is estimated that there are from 10-20 times as many suicide attempts as suicide deaths. And already in this new century, there have been more than five million suicide deaths worldwide. Each year approximately one million people in the world die by suicide.* **This toll is higher than the total number of world deaths each year from war and homicide combined."**

And these figures would be much higher if we included all of the instances where these things happen but never got reported. Also, they don't include the enormous number of people who are just very unhappy because they are lonely, in a relationship that is not going well, don't make enough money to pay their bills, have jobs they really dislike with no hope of ever doing better, suffer from some debilitating illness, are elderly without resources, etc., etc., etc.

Hopefully, this information will help you realize that most of the people you come in contact with everyday—regardless of how they appear—are not really ok. That their actual lives may be far from what they imagined it might be and that they experience much more suffering than you would ever imagine. This knowledge will help you to have more compassion for others when they behave in a way that, previously you would have thought of as 'bad.' Now you can see that, like all of the rest of us, given their life circumstances and conditioning, they are simply unable to do any better. Life is tough and we are simply not always able to do the right thing.

One of the projects our community is working for is to have one day each year declared National Tolerance day. This would be a day where everyone went about their day as usual, but whenever they encountered any negativity, they would simply let it go. Someone cuts you off in traffic...so what. Another person says something rude...so what. As soon as it happens, it's forgotten. Everyone would attempt to not react from their conditioning and get angry or irritated. We know that once people begin to experience the magic that happens when you show someone who is in a negative state compassion instead of anger, it will have a profound effect on the consciousness of the population in general.

The above statistics show that most of us need help, but of course, in our society, asking for help is too often equated with failure, so we rarely do it. Regardless of our circumstances, we attempt to always appear as if we are just fine. However, even without someone asking for help, we can give it. Showing compassion to others who find themselves acting badly is one way we can begin to help each other. Instead of getting angry with someone you see who is upset, remaining in your OO and asking if there is anything you can do for them is another.

Everyone, without exception, at times (much more than you may believe and much more than they are willing to allow anyone to see) experiences fear, anxiousness, loneliness, despair, depression, and every other negative emotion. Truly understanding this will allow you to treat others with far more tolerance and compassion.

Myth #5 - Love and acceptance are two different things.

"Your task is not to seek love, but merely to seek and find all the barriers within yourself that you have built against it." ~ Rumi

For many people, loving someone is one thing, and accepting them quite another. This stems from the fact that normally, rather than being in love with the actual person, we are in love with some idealized version of them we have created in our mind. We accept the parts of their personality that please us and try to get them to change those that don't. In other words, we want them to act in a way that pleases us all the time. This is indeed love, but for one's self, not the other.

To 'love' someone when they are doing what you want is easy, but the real test of your love is how well you are able to accept your partner when they are not pleasing you. I don't mean having affairs or beating you, obviously those things are not acceptable.

159

But to say you love someone and then push and prod them, attempt to manipulate them emotionally to become your ideal is not love at all.

Examples of this are: "You love him, but wish he was more motivated, more ambitious." or "You love her, but wish she would lose some weight." or "You love him, but wish he was not so sloppy." or "You love her, but wish she was not so emotional." or "You love him, but wish he would not spend so much time watching television." or "You love her, but wish she would spend less time with her family." or "You love him, but wish he was more romantic." The list is endless and usually includes multiple things we wish our partner would do differently...*to please us.*

There are those who love and feel they can never do enough for their beloved. There are others who say they love you but feel you never do enough for them. This first group will always see the best in you, the second group the worst. The first group is always aware of others feelings and could never intentionally hurt anyone, the second lacks this merciful awareness and so regularly hurts others while closing their eyes to what they have done. For them, others pain—like anything not having to do directly with themselves—just doesn't matter very much.

They cause an ocean of suffering and imagine it is but a drop. So preoccupied are they with their needs and their wants and their troubles that other's pain is barely noticed, if seen at all. Anyone would at this point want to know to which group they belong. How to tell?

Your capacity for selfless giving is the best indicator. Is the relationship for you about giving...or just getting? If you want to know the truth simply ask yourself if you are constantly ready to give everything to your beloved, or instead do you secretly resent the very idea of having to give and find yourself chronically unhappy because of what you feel you have not yet received from the relationship? From what has been said, your true nature and quality of your love can be easily known...you just have to be willing to see it.

Assuming that you wish to be more like the first group what must you do? The initial thing, as always, is to see through the eyes of your OO what aspects of your behavior falls into the second group. You must be willing to see a weak area before you can begin to do anything about it.

There is an extremely effective exercise that couples can do to help them move away from a lack of acceptance and toward a greater capacity to love. It must be done while both of you are in your OO and you carefully watch for any conditioning that may be triggered. Remember, you can always sense it is your conditioning which is rising by the emotional charge that accompanies it.

Here is what you would do; you sit down together and explain that you have this ideal picture of who you think the other should be. This must be done without any judgment of your partner. When you are explaining your expectations to the other person it must be clear that you are simply describing what you have seen about yourself and that you wish to let go of these expectations and learn to love them exactly as they are. Then your significant other does the same. Again, being clear that what they are describing is actually about something that they want to let go of. After you have both finished, you would each say to the other "My goal here is to learn to accept you and love you just the way you are."

Writing that phrase on the refrigerator or somewhere where you will both be able to see is constantly is a very good idea. Also, there should be a firm commitment to say to each other at least once a day "I love you, and my goal is to love you even better by learning to accept you just the way you are."

You will discover after doing this that the next time one of you feels the temptation to criticize the other that it will feel different. It will have lost some of its power over you and you will remember the discussion you had (and if you don't, the other will remind you) and the conversation will shift from whatever it was you were going to complain about, to the previous discussion of acceptance. Because you are now dealing with the real source of the problem (where one or the other of you is in a place of judgment—showing a lack of acceptance—toward the other) and operating from a more conscious state, you will no longer get lost in arguments discussing each other's inadequacy, but instead focus on each person's ability to be more accepting and loving.

This exercise can help each of you see, not only the judgments you place on the other, *but on yourself as well.* It can allow you to see conditioning that you had never been conscious of before. For example, thinking that you are very motivated and believing he should be too! Seeing this tells you that there is some conditioning around this whole idea of someone being motivated. The person making this judgment may find that they not only judge their partner too harshly, but themselves as well.

Turning the subject of the judgment into a question, such as "Do I expect too much of myself in terms of my work habits?" may reveal something previously unseen. Perhaps underneath all of that drive is a sense of inadequacy that pushes you to be too hard on yourself and causes you to *need* to overdo in an attempt to prove to yourself it is not really true.

One of the things that cause us to hold onto our conditioning is by seeing this behavior as a positive aspect of our personality. People with feelings of inadequacy feel very good about becoming overachievers (as I did), even though it is just one extreme in their personality pushing them to go to the other. People who are actually quite fearful, enjoy being aggressive, again for the same reason. The list of possible opposites working in people is quite extensive.

The previous exercise can allow you to see where you are left of center. That is, acting in one extreme or the other and then projecting those same unrealistic expectations you have for yourself on those around you. But of course, you have to be willing to see it, to move to your OO and really look at any extreme behavior and begin to see it more objectively.

Instead of this 'problem' pushing you further and further apart, this new way of dealing with it—with more love and acceptance—will bring you closer together and strengthen your relationship. You will realize the truth, that loving someone is best demonstrated by one's ability to accept them in their totality, and understand that loving and accepting are not two different things. The real secret is to realize with the deepest part of your being that one can only get to peace and happiness through acceptance and love.

However, you must also keep in mind that no one is capable of accepting another just as they are completely without doing this work for some time, that it is a process. Something you work at and become a little better at doing each day. So be patient with each other as you do this most kind and loving work.

Changing your thinking will be an absolutely necessary part of this process and it will help if you remember that you are always exactly as happy as you THINK you are. This of course applies to all areas of your life. Your relationship will be just as good as you THINK it is, your significant other will be just as good for you as you THINK they are, etc. It is quite possible to be surrounded by love but imagine it otherwise. The simple secret to ever-greater happiness is to simply forget about yourself as often as you can and instead think loving thoughts about someone else. The way to ever-greater unhappiness is easily found by doing just the opposite.

We all—every one of us, without exception—have our 'stuff.' When I was younger and understood little in regard to life I wished for someone without baggage. Now that I am older and my understanding of life is far greater, I no longer wish for—or would want—someone completely lacking issues (there is no one like that to be found anyway). How would I ever know if they truly loved me? Rather, my wish is for someone who has 'stuff' (just as I do) but who loves me enough—has the strength of character and courage—to see (and in that seeing become free of) it. There is no greater proof of one's love than in their willingness to partake in this type of 'seeing.'

Myth #6 - Romantic love is what makes life worth living and will bring us real happiness.

"If you are incapable of truly loving another and have been loved in kind you know madness.

If you are capable of truly loving another and have loved someone lacking this capacity, you are no stranger to either pain or loneliness.

If you are capable of truly loving another and have experienced the greatest of miracles...being loved in kind, you know bliss."
~ James LaFerla

This notion that romantic love makes life worth living and will bring you real happiness, has, is, and will be responsible for immeasurable unhappiness and pain. Earlier we discussed how, as children we experience certain emotional states (which result from chemical changes in our body) repeatedly and then become addicted to them. So, what most people mean when they tell you that they love you is that they have recognized (unconsciously of course) that you will enable them to feel those same emotional states (satisfy their body's addiction) they felt in their youth.

We grow up in a society where it is simply accepted that we 'fall in love' with someone without any need to really understand why. We're in love, it's wonderful, and that's enough. *I can't even begin to imagine how much unnecessary suffering could be avoided by a change in the way we view 'falling in love.'* What if instead of the way we see it now, we decided it was necessary, in fact, essential, to understand the real reason for our compelling feeling to be with another person.

We know from experience, our own and countless others, that the feeling of being in love with another is not a very good guide and can easily lead us into a situation that will cause us great pain. And yet, in spite of all of this evidence to the contrary, we continue to go with those feelings, never truly understanding what is happening.

If we were brought up in a home completely free of dysfunction where those around us were capable of loving us consciously, that is selflessly, then when we went out into the world, this mechanism that causes us to feel love for someone who will treat us as we were by our family, would work great.

Unfortunately, that is not what happens. Instead, we're brought up by parents who were less than perfect, and have life experiences that range from slightly, to severely traumatic. Whatever the circumstances, it is what we became used to and we will be powerfully drawn to anyone who will allow us to feel all of those feelings again. And we will call that feeling of being intensely attracted to another person 'love.'

We all say that we want to be happy and find someone that will treat us with love and consideration. What's important here is to realize that, *that's what your mind says*. Your body has other plans. It wants to feel all of the emotions it became used to when you were a child, even if they are quite painful. It will help you greatly in your next selection of a partner if you understand, really understand that *it's your body who normally decides.*

The 17th century philosopher René Descartes promoted the idea that the mind and body are separate, each completely disconnected from each other. Unfortunately, this concept was believed to be absolutely true until very recently. Now, that we know better, his philosophy has come to be known as "Descartes' error." His philosophy contributed greatly to the misconception that our mind is the captain of our ship, so to speak, and should somehow be able to exercise control over the brain and body, essentially how we behave. Many people still believe this to be true and it is partly responsible for their buying into Myth #1, the ideas that everyone is perfectly capable of changing their behavior and always doing the 'right' thing, if they really wanted to.

A more enlightened view can be found in a quote by Antonio Damasio, Professor of Neurology at the University of Iowa School of Medicine from his book "Descartes' Error: Emotion, Reason, and the Human" *"Although I cannot tell for certain what sparked my interest in the neural underpinnings of reason, I do know when I became convinced that the traditional views on the nature of rationality could not be correct. I had been advised early in life that sound decisions came from a cool head...I had grown up accustomed to thinking that the mechanisms of reason existed in a separate province of the mind, where emotion should not be allowed to intrude, and when I thought of the brain behind that mind, I envisioned separate neural systems for reason and emotion...but now I had before my eyes the coolest, least emotional, intelligent human being one might imagine, and yet his practical reason was so impaired that it produced, in the wanderings of daily life, a succession of mistakes, a perpetual violation of what would be considered socially appropriate and personally advantageous."*

What Professor Damasio is describing is the limitations of our mind and its ability to consistently and effectively regulate our behavior. In his book he describes how his research let him to the conclusion, based on the latest neurobiological research, that the mind isn't in control and that our behavior is really the result of our mind, brain, and body functioning as one integrated whole, with each part influencing the other.

His research confirms what I have experienced with myself and others repeatedly, that the mind, brain, and body are one, with the body—more often than not—'deciding' what the brain thinks. Our body feels hunger, we think about food. Our body is thirsty, we think about quenching that thirst. Alter your body chemistry in any way and your thinking will change. Our thoughts stem from whatever is happening in the body, including all that it has experienced in the past.

If our mind was in charge, why would we ever have an unhappy thought? Why wouldn't we just decide to do whatever we want and then always be able to follow through (such as diet, or quit smoking?). Once the body becomes addicted to something, for example, the emotions (chemical reactions) we experienced in our youth, it can be extremely difficult to think in a way that is inconsistent with that addiction and change the related behavior.

We can see this happening with others all the time; women who are beaten, yet stay with their mate, relationships where both parties are miserable but remain together. There are countless couples where one or the other feels unloved, unappreciated, experiences constant rejection, endures intense angry outbursts from the other, yet on they go.

And what's especially interesting is that, when one of these couples finally does separate, the individuals involved invariably find themselves in the same situation as before with their new partner. These people know intellectually that they are unhappy, but their mind provides no match for their bodies need to feel again the emotions of their youth, what they have come be believe is love.

If someone was able to see this feeling of 'love' for what it really is, an almost irresistible invitation to revisit the melodramas of our youth, their chances of finding real happiness would be increased dramatically.

What follows is a typical example of two people 'falling in love.' We start with a woman who as a child was treated severely by her father; her perception of him is that he was not a nice man, often angry and never very caring or considerate. Now she goes out into the world looking for a mate. Because of her conditioning she will be looking for a man very different from her father, someone she is absolutely sure is not like him at all. Eventually she meets a fellow who seems to be not just nice, but very, very nice.

She is immediately attracted to him and they begin a relationship. What she doesn't know however, is that her new partner appeared very, very nice because he was overcompensating for actually being rather cold and insensitive. Or that she was drawn to him because she had, as a result of her conditioning, lost her capacity to be objective. She was compelled to find someone who appeared to be extremely nice because of her reaction to her father's harsh behavior.

After the honeymoon phase of the relationship passes, she will begin to discover his true nature and find that she is once again with a man who treats her (allows her to feel the same emotional states) that her father did. She will re-experience the unhappiness she felt as a small girl but have a difficult time ending the relationship. What we can see from this is that it is **the body and its need to re-experience all of the emotions it felt as a child that is running the show.** Psychologically she is unhappy, but physiologically her body is getting just what it wants.

In order to avoid this type of dysfunctional partner selection, one must first let go of the romantic notions we all have about love. We have to understand what those feelings really are, and then we must become aware of the conditioning that unconsciously drives us to repeat our childhood melodramas. Until this conditioning is seen, at least partially, we are all helpless to avoid being controlled by it and will continue picking exactly the wrong mate.

The problem is that this feeling of being in 'love' is intoxicating. We lose our objectivity, we just want to be with the object of our love and our rational mind is normally no match for those powerful feelings we experience at those moments. Someone once said, "Choosing a mate while in the state of love is not unlike choosing an attorney while intoxicated."

Only by going to your OO and seriously considering what has been said, seeing how it has affected your past relationships and knowing—without a doubt—that those same dynamics are waiting to repeat themselves in your next relationship can you begin to develop the strength to maintain anything remotely resembling objectivity, the next time you find yourself smitten.

A friend, or group of friends, who are also involved in this work, can be a tremendous source of help. It will be easier for them to see what you may not yet be able to see for yourself, and just talking with them about someone you're considering having, or already in a relationship with can help immensely. Of course, you have to be willing to hear what they have to say. Listening while in your OO will make this much easier.

In addition to the tendency to 'fall in love' with someone who will probably make us unhappy, there is another problem which occurs during our selection of a mate. It happens because most of us think of ourselves as one singular person. But the truth is that we are really a composite of all of the pairs of personalities we accumulated growing up. We are much more like a group than one consistent individual. There are times when we feel like exercising and times when we don't. Sometimes we are happy with ourselves and our lives, and sometimes we feel just the opposite, one part of us wants to diet and another wants to over eat. The same is true of everyone else. So when someone says they love you, understand that it is but one part of their personality that feels this way and *that there will be others that will at times feel quite different.*

This knowledge gives us an edge. Instead of simply reacting to the person who says they love you as if that is how they will feel consistently from now on, we know the situation is more complicated. We can study their personality from our OO and see what other pairs of personalities will be joining the party later on. This bit of research can save us a great deal of subsequent suffering.

We must also examine ourselves in this process. Asking yourself why you love this person would be a good place to start. Are you just drawn to them for some reason of which you are unaware? If so, it is almost certainly your conditioning at work. Remember, feedback from friends who are capable of observing from their OO and have done a certain amount of inner work can be very valuable in this process.

One must return to the time of their youth mentally and attempt to remember in as much detail as possible what their relationship was like with their mother and father. Conversations with your siblings (if you have any) can provide valuable insight. Once you have accumulated this information, the next step is to look at it from your OO. Were one or both of your parents overly strict and did they treat you with disapproval on a regular basis?

Can you see any relationship between that behavior and the mates you have chosen in the past who wind up making you feel the same way? Possibly you lost one of your parents as a result of death or divorce. How did you feel when this happened and what impact do you see this as having on your choice of partners?

If you continue to look through your OO, you will begin to see a pattern emerge. You will begin to see what type of person you are unconsciously drawn to because of your conditioning and finally be able to see this 'attraction' for what it really is. This will be the beginning of your freedom to more consciously choose a mate that will actually make you happy rather than simply assist you in reliving the unhappiness of your childhood.

Another problem that you will encounter in this process is overcoming the desire to feel what you believed was love before. Attempting to have a relationship with someone who does not trigger all of your childhood conditioning, however capable they are of loving you, may not *feel* like love to you. You will have to approach the relationship differently and come to appreciate the love of someone capable of actually making you happy, even though it does not provide the same intense emotional pull that you would have felt before. This is a huge hurdle that some will find difficult to surmount. The desire to feel those feelings (what we formerly thought of as love) will be very powerful. This again is where a strong support group can help, as can rereading this chapter again as often as you need to be reminded of what is really happening.

One more difficulty is that when you are making your selection as you normally would, it all happens automatically. You don't really think about it. You meet someone; there is that unconscious recognition that they will play out your childhood melodramas and you find yourself 'in love.' When you attempt to avoid selecting a partner in this way it will be confusing at first. There won't be the intense emotional attraction and you will actually have to, consciously, using your OO, come to see who this person you are considering having a relationship with really is. It will require you to figure out which prospective partner actually would be a healthy, happy, supportive, loving companion.

Since you will be new at this, it will feel awkward at first. You must take a conscious look at your life and come to understand better what type of person, with which type of traits would be a good choice. We offer Couple Compatibility consultations that can help you see more clearly, if you are going to be happy with your choice.

Keep in mind that the vast majority of people are still run by their conditioning and will bring all of their baggage with them to the relationship. They will have negative behavior that they are unaware of, there will be patterns of dysfunction, and a tendency to project the behavior they received from their parents growing up on to you at times.

While no one is perfect, it will certainly improve your chances for making a good choice if you find someone else engaged in, or willing to become engaged in this work, who understands, at least to a degree, the problems their conditioning causes them and has done a certain amount of work to free themselves from it.

When you see someone who is 'fixed,' that is, unwilling to look within themselves and see their flaws and has no desire to improve themselves, understand that they will be extremely difficult to work with in solving any problem you encounter. They will see the problems you have as a couple as always being *your* problems and any chance for a resolution to whatever problems you do have will be virtually impossible.

For you to have any chance for lasting happiness in the relationship, the other person must have some idea of what real love is. They should be able to answer the following questions correctly. When your conditioning causes you to be impatient or irritated with the object of our love, is that love? When your conditioning causes you to think badly of the object of your love, is that love? When our conditioning causes you to feel anger, resentment, or anything other than love, is that love? Of course not. So in the end it becomes clear what is the greatest barrier to really loving another...ones very own conditioning, our precious self with all of its petty emotions and selfishness. One's ability to love is in direct proportion to their ability to let go of their conditioning. This will be true for yourself as well as your mate.

Myth #7 - That there is anyone to blame for our lives and the problems we have.

"All blame is a waste of time. No matter how much fault you find with another, and regardless of how much you blame him, it will not change you. The only thing blame does is to keep the focus off you when you are looking for external reasons to explain your unhappiness or frustration. You may succeed in making another feel guilty about something by blaming him, but you won't succeed in changing whatever it is about you that is making you unhappy."
~ Wayne Dyer

We could say all of our problems are because of the conditioning we received from our parents and that it is their fault, feel sorry for ourselves, and use that as an excuse to behave badly in the future. But then we would have to say no, it is *their* parents fault for bringing them up the way they did. And again, we would have to keep going back to each previous generation endlessly. There is, in fact, no one to blame. Things have happened the way they have in your, and everyone else's, life for one reason, a lack of consciousness about who we really are and the tools to change. Because of the Quickening that is happening now and the methods for change that are emerging, our generation has the potential to turn this wave after wave (generation after generation) of dysfunction into something quite different.

The real responsibility lies within each individual to begin seeing the true source of their problems by being willing to look within themselves. The Quickening is increasing everyone's power to do this and more and more techniques are becoming available to help. The only question is, do you want to continue going through life with the unseen forces from your conditioning causing you to live your life constantly making the same mistakes, suffering uselessly, and never realizing your true potential. Or are you willing to do the work necessary to change all of that?

Myth #8 - Our negative emotions are the responsibility of someone other than ourselves.

"Taking responsibility means never blaming anyone else for anything you are being, doing, having, or feeling." ~ Susan Jeffers

When one finally is able to see that no one is responsible for their negative emotions other than themselves, they will have taken one of the biggest steps on their path to higher consciousness. In fact, I will say that, until one let's go of this myth, very little, if any progress can be made. That is because as long as we continue to blame others for what is essentially our unique response to various life situations, we can never begin changing that response and so will remain stuck.

There is an unconscious expectation built into this myth. It says, "If everyone would just be nice and treat me the way I think they should, I wouldn't get upset." Anyone who stops and thinks about this for a minute will realize what this means. That in order for us to avoid getting angry, the world would have to be perfect. And more than that, everyone would always behave in the manner in which we believe they should.

Obviously, this is never going to happen and puts all of the control of our emotions in the hands of whatever person, or persons, we might encounter. This unconscious idea that other people are responsible for our negative emotions develops in us because we have all grown up in a world where we see people continually blaming their anger, irritation, frustration, etc. on others and then quite naturally begin doing the same ourselves. And of course, it feels much better to blame someone other than ourselves.

There is another phenomenon, which acts to cause us to judge others harshly and become negative toward them. It results from judgments we have about ourselves that we may or may not be aware of and project onto others. For example, someone may have received some rather intense conditioning as a child related to what is 'right' and what is 'wrong' and was severely punished when they didn't do the 'right' thing.

This conditioning then becomes a part of this person's thinking causing them to internalize the values of their parent or parents who judged them so harshly and now judge others in this same way. They will, without realizing it of course, continue being too hard on themselves for the rest of their life. And until they are able to stop judging themselves so severely they will never be able to stop judging others the same way.

There are many other examples where the extreme conditioning we received as a child becomes part of our belief system and causes us, and others to suffer. Perhaps your parents were very impatient with you when it came to doing whatever they asked and now you continue to do the same to yourself—*and others*. Did they make you feel incompetent and so you overcompensate by setting the bar too high for yourself—*and others?* Or maybe your parents instilled in you the belief that anyone who didn't go to church regularly, believe in God, or who was not a Christian was 'bad.'

There are an enormous number of possibilities of the various conditioning one can receive, internalized, and then project on others and cause us to become irritated or angry with them.

One of the difficulties with becoming aware of this dynamic in yourself is that you may see your response to the conditioning you received as positive. In the above examples for instance, the impatient person who pushes themselves too hard may see this behavior as something that has made them more capable than others. The overachiever may see their pushing themselves too hard as a good thing, something which has helped them advance quickly in their work. And the church going individual may enjoy the feeling of being a very good Christian.

And, of course, there is nothing wrong with trying to be a good Christian, but when we take it to the extreme and judge others harshly who do not believe as we do, there is nothing Christian about that at all.

What's really important to see here is that each of these individuals was made to feel a certain way, for example incompetent, and they are now driven to spend the rest of their life going to the other extreme. *Not because they have any choice, but because they are compelled to do it. This is not them acting consciously, just an automatic response to the conditioning they received growing up.* Not living up to their parent's expectations felt very uncomfortable and, in order to get rid of this 'discomfort' (the judgment they internalized) they are forced to be impatient with themselves, overachieve, or over believe.

Seeing, through the eyes of your OO the things which make you angry with other people can be a wonderful way to begin seeing things about yourself. There is an old saying that the world is a mirror. If you see someone who complains regularly about someone else's ego, there is an excellent chance their own ego is the problem. Listen to someone who constantly complains about others being lazy, and you can be sure that they were subject to

176

this same sort of judgment as a child and still judge themselves as lazy unless they overdo. If we begin to look for the true cause of our anger *within ourselves,* it can be very enlightening, and then when we are able to deal with the real source and begin freeing ourselves from it, very liberating. Remember, any sort of judgment about the behavior of others always comes from your conditioning...*and tells you much more about yourself than about anyone else.*

As you begin to see yourself and others through the eyes of your OO, you will come to understand what many fail to see, *that you have a choice.* **That no one can make you feel anything without your permission.** This realization is enormous. That is, once you see that you can allow yourself to react to the various situations that occur in your life from your conditioning, reflexively with some negative emotion, or, you can choose instead to simply see what is happening and not descend into some negative state.

Once you have started choosing for yourself to react from a more conscious place, you will have taken a hard right turn from what your life would have normally been from that point on and started down another path that will bring you more and more control over your emotions and ever increasing peace. Taking responsibility for your negative emotions puts the control back in your hands, gives you great freedom, and allows you to handle the situations you encounter in life in a very different—more objective and productive—way.

Occasionally, during one of my seminars when I bring up this topic someone will ask me a question like "So are you saying if I was walking down the street with my wife and someone came up and punched her in the face I shouldn't get mad?" My response is to ask them if this sort of thing happens to them often." Invariably they will so no. So I then ask, "Well, what sorts of things do happen that cause you to become upset?" The usual answers to this are "When my boss does this..." or my "Wife says or does that..." or

"When someone is rude to me in traffic." Now we have gotten back to dealing with real life situations, not some extreme situation which will probably never occur and allows us to put everything back into perspective.

When I ask additional questions to investigate the thinking that results in their being angry, we can always connect it back to their conditioning. For instance, when he was a child, one or both of his parents treated him like he was stupid a good deal of the time. Now, when his wife makes any comment, which could be taken as criticism, he overreacts and becomes upset. Again, we see that it is not the situation that is happening in the present that is the problem, but rather his conditioned response which is to react too strongly to anything that feels to him like someone is once again saying he is stupid (because some part of him still believes he is).

Nothing his wife could ever do, short of constantly walking on eggshells and being extremely careful about any comment she might make, would keep him from having this reaction over and over again. And, of course, expecting her to act that way would be unreasonable and would never help him correct his conditioned hypersensitivity to criticism. Only he can do that by using his OO to 'see' rather than 'be' that conditioning.

Remember, whenever we find ourselves in a negative state, it is always because we are acting from our conditioning. We are reacting to what happened to us in the past, not dealing with what is happening in the present in a more objective and conscious way.

When we become negative, a whole host of chemicals flood our body. Our objectivity disappears; our ability to think clearly is severely decreased. We can't even breathe right when we are upset. Another down side to getting angry is that the more often we do it, the more often those chemicals spread through our bodies, the more we predispose ourselves to illness. It has been proven conclusively that people who are in negative states regularly have dramatically higher incidences of ulcers, heart disease, high blood pressure, cancer, and other diseases.

There will be those individuals who find it difficult to express their feelings. They tend to be too permissive and consistently give in to the wishes of others, though they may want to do something else. As you know from our earlier discussion, all personalities develop in pairs. For the individual we are describing, being too passive is one extreme. What's the other? Can you guess? It is at times becoming very upset and expressing their feelings, but with far too much intensity. This angry extreme where they finally get to express their sense of being taken advantage of and not considered by others, feels to them like they are no longer afraid and passive, but finally in a position of strength and power. They actually enjoy those moments. These people will see not expressing their anger as a sentence to continually live in a position where they are weak, never being able to express their true feelings.

So what is the answer? Should they continue to get very angry at times or remain constantly passive. The correct answer is neither. One extreme in them (their intense anger) is the result of the other (their general passivity). Only by working through their OO and beginning to substitute their passivity with the ability to, without becoming upset, express their desires will they ever reach that center objective place between one extreme and the other.

I could describe many other scenarios brought about by someone's conditioning that results in their feeling the actual need to be angry at times. Hopefully the previous example will show that anger is always a result of one's conditioning and eliminates their ability to live in balance. One must come to see their negative emotions as an affliction, rather than a positive part of their personality and begin to work to rid themselves of it as they would any other dysfunction.

And finally, it is important to understand that behind all anger, its real source, is fear. We could talk about all of the different types of fears, but they can all be reduced to essentially two. Fear for your personal safety, and by far the most common fear, the fear of loss of love. While it is very easy to see where one would react to fear of personal injury, it can be difficult to see the connection between anger and loss of love.

A few examples will help. Take the man who gets angry with his wife or significant other when she disagrees with him. What is really going on is that he feels as if she sees him as incompetent, her feelings for him may change from love and respect to something else. Then there is the wife who gets upset when her husband says something that can be taken as a criticism of how she looks. To her it feels that she may no longer be attractive to him and so will lose his love. Children often respond to disapproval from their parents with anger, equating that disapproval with a loss of their parents love.

Getting back now to the fear for your personal safety. The natural reaction is of course fear. But is it the best one? Does it help us deal with that situation most effectively? The answer is no. When you become frightened and then angry, your body and mind simply don't function at an optimum level. This response actually decreases our chance of surviving the situation. It is a response still with us from when we might encounter some beast in the woods that saw us as dinner. The extreme fight or flight response was appropriate then, but not many of us find ourselves needing to defend ourselves from a man eating whatever.

I competed very successfully in full contact Karate for many years. I attribute much of that success to my ability to control my normal conditioned response in those situations. I used my OO to simply see and respond to what was happening. My response was always faster and more correct than it would have been otherwise. It was always the person who allowed their emotions to get the best of them—who became angry—that lost.

180

Most people go through their entire lives never realizing that their negative responses to situations have much more to do with the past than with the present. That they are not so much responding to life now in a conscious way, but rather simply reacting reflexively from their past experiences. They were conditioned to respond that way, and now believe it is just who they are. It may be who someone, without their say so, made them, but it certainly doesn't have to be who they remain.

Your ability to see the conditioning that results in your responding in a negative way and moving away from it, will be the single greatest indicator that you are making progress toward becoming more conscious.

Myth #9 - That somehow punishing someone brings about a positive change in them.

"Where did we ever get the crazy idea that in order to make someone do better, first we have to make them feel worse? Think of the last time you felt humiliated or treated unfairly. Did you feel like cooperating or doing better?" ~ Jane Nelson

Our prison system and the statistics showing the number of repeat offenders—all who have been punished—proves this myth to be completely false. We sentence people to death—kill them—and then tell others not to kill. We put people in situations where they are treated inhumanely (in prisons) and then expect them to somehow become more humane.

While there are those individuals who, due to their dysfunctional conditioning or some physiological problem, need to be separated from the general population, they should be seen, not as bad or evil, but simply as victims of the conditions they grew up in or their genetics. Rather than locking them away in a cell and forgetting about them, we should see them as someone who needs help and we should do everything possible to assist them to become functional members of our society. In some cases, we may not succeed, but that doesn't mean we shouldn't try.

Helping to bring someone to a place of higher consciousness makes it possible for them to see what they were incapable of seeing before, their effect on others and as a result, how inappropriate their actions were. They will become changed. The greater their consciousness, the less their capacity for doing anything that would cause another harm. Increased consciousness always results in an increased capacity to love and have compassion for others. Treating someone as though they are bad, labeling them that way and then putting them in a cell with other 'bad' people has just the opposite effect.

Someone once said, *"As long as we believe in prisons, we will need them."* This statement is not only true, but tells us that it is the very idea that we should punish, rather than help others, that keeps our present ineffectual penal system in place. When someone acts in a way that is socially unacceptable, we tend to see them as bad. This completely false idea must be replaced by a more conscious and compassionate view. Punishing someone only perpetuates the problem by causing more resentment and anger. They may afterwards comply with the rules, at least for a time, but only out of fear, not because they have changed. What's needed instead is for someone to help them develop a new understanding—to actually change—and enable them to live their life from a more conscious place.

Instead of a war against crime, we should be engaged in a war against dysfunctional conditioning, starting with ourselves and our children. If our focus changed and we proceeded in this way, many children who would otherwise grow up to commit crimes would not, drastically reducing the next generation of crime without the need for more police, more guns, and more prisons. And if we began treating those adults who are simply seen as criminals instead as people who need help to change their lives and become more functional, that too would significantly reduce the numbers of repeat offenders and the need for more police, more guns, and more prisons. Our world and the amount of crime happening in it would begin to change dramatically. But this can only happen if we see the situation from this higher place of consciousness, which thanks to the Quickening is now becoming possible.

Can you think of times in your life where you caused another pain who was undeserving of your anger? Or a time when you committed some act which hurt someone who had done nothing to you? Should you have been punished in some way for what you did? Would it have helped? Or is it more likely that the only reason you haven't continued to do such things (which is hopefully the case) is because your feelings have changed? You became more conscious, that is, saw *and felt* the pain you caused this other person, and as a result simply weren't capable of doing it again.

From this example, it can be easily seen what is necessary to help someone who acts in a way that causes others to suffer. By now, it should be obvious that punishment will never *change* them. Only by their becoming more conscious and as a result experiencing what they were incapable of before—truly seeing— and as a result *feeling* the pain they caused others, only then will it have any lasting effect.

I am in the process of writing another book devoted entirely to this topic which will be offered free of charge to any prison library who will accept it. It will provide the tools and information needed for those who have found themselves in this terrible circumstance to see their behavior for what it is and allow them to begin changing so they never have to experience that situation again.

Myth #10 - That because someone looks different than us, wears another type of clothing, has another color skin, speaks another language, or is from another country that they are somehow different from us.

"Our judgments judge us, and nothing exposes us, reveals our weaknesses, more ingeniously than our own opinion of others."
~ James LaFerla

This idea stems from our tendency to look only at the superficial and not see that there is an actual person underneath their external appearance with all of the hopes and fears we feel, a person who, like us, experiences both happiness and suffering in their life. However, you might perceive someone as different from yourself, at our core we are all essentially the same. We all want to love and be loved. People may express themselves differently than you, but we are all born knowing someday we are going to die, we all feel a great deal of fear, sadness, loneliness, heartbreak, and despair at times in our lives.

This objectifying of others allows us to treat them, at the very least with disregard, and at the extreme, with hatred, and has been responsible for incalculable suffering. The Germans during World War II saw the Jews as being very different from themselves, which allowed them to commit unspeakably horrific acts, including torture and mass genocide. In our own country, for hundreds of years, blacks were treated more like livestock than actual human beings and suffered terrible prejudice and brutality.

Even now, as I write these words, people are waging war and killing each other in Ireland, Bosnia, Serbia, Palestine and many other places, simply because they are incapable of seeing past their differences and instead realizing just how much more similar than not we all are. **Whenever anyone of us sees someone in this way—when we react to only their appearance—*we ourselves are contributing to, and actually perpetuating this process.***

This is an area where our conditioning comes into play very strongly. We grow up in world where we often adopt the views of those around us. If you were brought up in a wealthy family, you may have developed certain negative feelings about the poor and perhaps think of them as somehow incompetent or lazy. If you were brought up in the Deep South, you may have been conditioned to think of blacks as inferior. Maybe your parents were white supremists and you find yourself uncomfortable around anyone who is not white. It is difficult to be raised in a world so full of prejudice and not be touched by it. Everyone is to some degree and most people never question their automatic reactions to those they see as different.

This way of seeing others is the product of fear resulting from a very low level of consciousness. You could ignore this dark tendency in yourself, or, using your OO, you could begin to watch your automatic conditioned response to those you come in contact with. You may be surprised at just how much judgment you see in yourself toward others.

What's your reaction to the guy dressed like a biker or someone sporting a few tattoos? Or if you happen to be a biker, what's your reaction to the next guy you encounter all dressed up in a business suit? How about someone who happens to be gay? Perhaps you encounter a person who looks like they could be from Iraq? Do you wonder if he might be somehow connected with terrorists and feel yourself becoming negative toward them? What about your feelings toward Mexicans, Chinese, or any other race?

We all develop stereotypes, which are often the result of what is called *attribute substitution*. This happens when we are required to make a judgment regarding something or someone that is very complex and refers to our tendency to attempt to simplify it, and is just one of a variety of techniques people use to reduce the effort involved in decision-making.

For example, when we meet someone for the first time, trying to judge their intelligence or true nature is much more difficult than simply making a decision based on the color of their skin or general appearance. This sort of prejudice happens unconsciously and via our intuitive judgment system, rather than from a more conscious place and allows someone to believe they have actually made an honest, unbiased evaluation of the other person. It also explains why people are often unaware of their own biases and why they persist even when someone does become aware of them.

It takes effort and real courage to be completely honest with yourself and work to change your conditioned view to one more conscious. The more you do it, the more you will see the insanity of all of us walking around judging so many others negatively, and begin to understand what the accumulative impact of this behavior has on our society. Seeing this—and that *you too are being judged constantly*—will help you move in the right direction. Away from an unconscious, negative reaction, toward one of increasing compassion, tolerance, and love for others.

Fifteen - The Mistaken View That There are 'Bad' or Evil People.

"The value of compassion cannot be over-emphasized. Anyone can criticize. It takes a true believer to be compassionate. No greater burden can be borne by an individual than to know no one cares or understands." ~ Arthur H. Stainback

From the time we are born we are subjected to the idea of their being 'good' guys and 'bad' guys. Any typical western movie is a perfect example. There were the good guys (us) and the bad guys (the Indians). We saw this sort of thing over and over again and simply came to accept the idea as fact.

If some aliens came here from another planet and decided they had 'discovered' earth and saw us as savages, we would see them as the bad guys. This situation is exactly the same as when Columbus 'discovered' America. He didn't discover it; it was already there populated by millions of Indians. Our idea of discovering it for ourselves and seeing the Indians as savages is no different from the previous example with the aliens. We decided this was now our property and the Indian's efforts to stop us from taking their home somehow made them the bad guys.

Not only did we kill untold numbers of Native Americans who were simply trying to protect their home land (exactly as we all would do today if invaded by aliens attempting to take over our world) but from the 16th through the early 20th century, no fewer than 93 confirmed epidemics and pandemics—all of which can be attributed to European contagions—decimated the American Indian population. Native American populations in the American Southwest plummeted by a staggering 90 percent or more. And still we saw them as the bad guys. Were they? Not at all, in fact, all of the facts suggest something quite different, that it was us who were the bad guys. The point being, labeling someone as 'bad' without knowing all the facts is extremely common and almost always leaves out any consideration of why they acted as they did.

Most of us have continued to hold on to this 'good buy' 'bad guy' philosophy. Today our jails are filled with what we all believe are 'bad' people. What is not considered is what brought these individuals to behave as they did that resulted in their incarceration. If we could see their lives from a place of objectivity and compassion, we would understand that the conditions of their youth, or some physiological defect predisposed them to the behaviors that resulted in their being imprisoned.

Suppose your father was a very violent man who treated you with violence and that is all you ever saw? No doubt, all of his attitudes about other people would become part of your belief system as well. As you got older and act out the violence that was heaped upon you, you suddenly find yourself in prison. There are countless other examples of how someone could grow up in violent, desperate circumstances and end up the same way.

In the 1980s, in an attempt to find the origins of antisocial personality disorders and their influence over crime, studies were conducted of twins and adopted children. It was already well know that identical twins have the exact same genetic makeup. What the results of the research found was that *identical twins were twice as likely to have similar criminal behavior than fraternal twins who have similar but not identical genes.* Additional research showed that adopted children had greater similarities of crime rates to their biological parents than to their adoptive parents, strongly suggesting *a genetic basis for some criminal behavior.*

As new advances are made in medical technology, our capacity for understanding the biological and biochemical causes of criminal behavior have became significantly more sophisticated. For instance, in 1986 psychologist Robert Hare identified a connection between certain brain activity and antisocial behavior. He found that criminals experienced less brain reaction to dangerous situations than most people. He believed that such brain function could lead to greater risk-taking in life, with some criminals not fearing punishment as much as others. A physical characteristic they never asked for, but rather just happen to inherit.

Studies related to brain activity and its relationship to criminal behavior has continued. We are now capable of testing with advanced instruments and probing the inner workings of the brain to a degree that was never before possible. With techniques called computerized tomography (CT scans), magnetic resonance imaging (MRI), and positron emission tomography (PET scans); researchers are able to search for links between brain activity and a tendency to commit crime.

Part of the research on brain activity was related to investigating the role of neurochemicals, those chemicals we mentioned earlier that the brain releases which affect the body, and how they might influence criminal behavior. It was found that increased levels of some neurochemicals, such as serotonin, actually decreases aggression. Serotonin is a powerful substance produced by the central nervous system that can dramatically affect ones emotional state. Higher levels of other neurochemicals, such as dopamine, increase aggression. Dopamine is produced by the brain and affects both the heart rate and blood pressure. These increased levels are, again, something one inherits rather than asks for.

Then there is the role of hormones, bodily substances that affect how organs in the body function like testosterone for example. Researchers found a relationship between hormones and criminal behavior. Testosterone, a sex hormone produced by male sexual organs that cause development of masculine body traits. Many animal studies have shown a strong link between high levels of testosterone and aggressive behavior. Testosterone measurements in prison populations also showed relatively high levels in the inmates as compared to the U.S. adult male population in general.

There have been studies of sex offenders in Germany, which showed testosterone to have a strong bearing on criminal behavior. It was discovered that those who were treated to remove testosterone as part of their sentencing became repeat offenders only 3 percent of the time, *a dramatic decrease from the usual 46 percent repeat rate.*

There is another hormone, cortisol, which has been linked to criminal behavior. High cortisol levels occur when someone's attention is focused or when they are physically active, whereas low levels of cortisol are associated with a shorter attention span, lesser activity levels, and are often connected to various types of antisocial behavior, including crime. Studies of violent adults have shown them to have lower levels of cortisol.

The latest technology which allows us to peer deeper into the workings of the brain than was ever before possible has shown us that the behavior of some criminals is related to actual physiological dysfunctions within their brains. The behavior of psychopaths is, in fact, quite similar to those patients with prefrontal brain damage. Improperly functioning brains maybe, at least in part, the cause of their behavior. Perhaps they do not have the capacity that keeps normal people from committing crimes.

If psychopaths are actually suffering from some sort of physiological defect, if their antisocial actions have a biological cause, shouldn't we treat them the way we would anyone else we discovered had brain damage? And those people who inherit higher than normal levels of hormones or have a neurochemical imbalance that is beyond their control and wind up committing crimes, how should we treat them? Obviously since some criminals are driven by factors largely out of their control, simply punishing them will not be an effective deterrent. Shouldn't help and proper treatment be given instead?

Simply labeling these people as 'bad' and putting them into a brutal environment lacking compassion does nothing to help them to overcome their dysfunctional childhood conditioning or correcting whatever physiological defect they may have inherited and begin to be capable of living more productive lives. Again, the statistics showing the number of repeat offenders proves this conclusively. What is needed instead, is to see these people who were victims as children, as human beings, still victims of their negative programming or defective physiology that are in need of help, real help to allow them to change the real cause of what they have become.

Treating these people as 'bad' that had such unhappy childhoods, ignoring the fact that all of that conditioning still causes them great suffering, and then providing, not help, but more punishment reflects the tremendous lack of consciousness in our society in general.

Less extreme examples involve people we meet every day at work, while driving, etc. We see someone that is frequently angry, aggressive, rude, or whatever and again label them as 'bad.' Hopefully what you have read so far and your ability to see yourself and others through the eyes of your OO is helping you to see that no one is acting badly consciously. That simply isn't possible. It is a contradiction in terms. In fact, the more conscious someone becomes, the less capable they are of treating others with anything other than love and compassion.

There are no 'bad' people. Only people who, due to the poor conditioning they received as a child or some physiological defect causes them to act at times in a way that society finds unacceptable. They suffered as children, they are suffering as adults, and what they deserve is our compassion and help, not hatred, anger, and more abuse.

No truly conscious person would ever choose to be unhappy or intentionally cause suffering for others. Perhaps you are beginning to see that people with this kind of conditioning—which we all have to some degree—are completely unaware of how inappropriate their conditioned response may be. To them, these feelings are correct. Just like the rest of us, they will believe that their conditioned reflexive response, that is, how they 'feel' about something is how everyone else should feel and have difficulty understanding why someone else would react differently. From this, it is easy to see how—as we come to accept our automatic reactions as 'right' without ever questioning them—our capacity for objectivity disappears. Along with this loss of objectivity, goes our ability to empathize, it becomes very difficult to relate to someone whose feelings are unlike our own (who has a different automatic response).

There are no 'bad' people, only people with 'bad' conditioning or some physiological defect, which unconsciously drives them to cause suffering for themselves and others, conditioning which they neither asked for nor agreed to accept. Our response to them should be one of awareness and compassion rather than harsh judgment, followed by our reacting with our own negative conditioning and perhaps doing something bad or evil ourselves, even if it's only in our mind.

Do you still believe there are bad people out there? Are there perhaps people who think or have thought of you as bad? Are you? Should you be thought of in that way because you did something that made someone else angry, because you have conditioning that, at times, causes you to act inappropriately by other's standards? And how should you be dealt with by those who think badly of you? And how do you think you should treat those you may still think of as bad?

There was a study done involving inmates on death row at a number of prisons. When asked if, whatever act had resulted in their being there, was their fault, each and every individual's response was the same; they all said their victims all did something bad, which drove them to harm them in some way. They all embraced this idea of their being bad people which then made it perfectly acceptable, in fact, compulsory that they kill them. The courts and the family's of the victims saw what they did quite differently.

This idea of there being 'bad' people is responsible for incalculable violence and murder. The moment we allow ourselves to think of anyone else in this way, rather than responding with tolerance and compassion, we diminish ourselves and make the world a little darker.

Sixteen - Really Understanding Others.

"Life has no other discipline to impose, if we would but realize it, than to accept life unquestioningly. Everything we shut our eyes to, everything we run away from, everything we deny, denigrate or despise, serves to defeat us in the end. What seems nasty, painful, evil can become a source of beauty, joy and strength, if faced with an open mind. Every moment is a golden one for him who has the vision to recognize it as such." ~ Henry Miller

It is extremely important to begin seeing that others are trapped in the conditioning they received in their youth, as are most people, and that, unless they are willing to take a critical look at their behavior, they are essentially fixed and will never change. Truly understanding this will allow us to interact with others more effectively. Too often, we engage others in conversations intended to show them how inappropriate we believe their behavior is and end up arguing. If you understand that your mother's critical nature is simply the result of her conditioning—not a conscious choice she has made—and see that this behavior is never going to change, no matter how often you discuss it or hope she will suddenly see the light. The same situation might exist with a father that is too angry, a brother that is too passive, a sister that repeatedly seeks out dysfunctional men to have relationships with, and friends that are too needy or too negative.

Seeing that there is nothing you can do to change them and beginning to let go of trying is a big step along the way to higher consciousness and an indicator that you are becoming freer of your conditioned, reactive response to them. Always remember that when you find yourself reacting with negativity to another, that you have descended back down into your conditioning. As you see this and work against it, irritation and anger will begin to be replaced with compassion and acceptance.

Instead of trying to change your relative's (or anyone else's) behavior so they act the way you think they should and don't do or say anything that you might find objectionable, you begin the process of simply letting them be who they are. You learn to accept them. This is a great way for you to measure your progress.

Your ever-increasing ability to be around this person without falling into some negative conditioning will be a very clear indicator that you are moving up our scale to a place of more consciousness. As you simply let go of any judgment regarding this person or their actions, you will find that other, much more positive emotions begin to appear. Your newfound ability to accept your friend or relative just as they are will bring you much closer together and avoid countless moments of suffering you would experience had you not made this transition. Always remember, real love and acceptance, are not two different things.

There is also another type of situation, which can occur where you find yourself holding on to a relationship with someone that is always unhappy, angry, or in need of help. If you find yourself in this circumstance, you might want to ask yourself why. Almost certainly, you will see that your conditioning is involved. Perhaps being around someone very dysfunctional makes you feel better about yourself. Do you have an exaggerated need to save others (which again, might make you feel better about yourself and keep you from seeing where you might need help?). Do you find that certain friends support certain negative attitudes you experience and that you are able to share them with each other? Watching from your OO will begin to help you see what this relationship is all about and if you really want to continue it.

Others will always act in ways that you find objectionable. As you become more conscious, you see this behavior as just part of who they are and your desire to do something about it will steadily diminish. You will just see that they, like everyone else, are a mixture of what could be call 'good' qualities and other less positive ones and learn to accept them just as they are.

In fact, you can measure your progress by your increasing ability to simply accept others—just as they are. *Loving someone is best demonstrated by one's ability to accept them in their totality. Understand that loving and accepting are not two different things.*

Of course, there will be those who are interested in change and whom you can help or who may be able to help you at times. But keep in mind that no one can ever be forced to change. We must be able to discriminate between those who are 'fixed' and those who are willing to engage in a sincere self-examination and are looking for way to change their life.

Seventeen - How to Drastically Reduce Your Children's Suffering Later in Life.

"Safety and security don't just happen; they are the result of collective consensus and public investment. We owe our children, the most vulnerable citizens in our society, a life free of violence and fear." ~ Nelson Mandela

We have seen how adult's lives are run mostly by the conditioning they received as children, and the devastating effect it can have on the quality of their life. We have also seen once one becomes an adult, having been that conditioning for 20, 30, 40 or more years, how difficult it can be to change. Wouldn't it be wonderful if you were able to go back and change the conditioning you received so that you were never again drawn to behavior that results in your suffering uselessly? **As parents, we have the opportunity to give this incredible gift to our children.** We can come to see how our conditioned behavior can predispose them to a lifetime of unhappiness and make a conscious decision to change this behavior and as a result dramatically alter the course of our children's lives for the better, beginning today.

What's required however is a complete review of our vision of how we interact with our children. It necessitates a great deal of courage and the willingness to take a more conscious look at our own conditioning, and see that some may be doing more harm than good. We will have to become aware of the patterns of behavior we experienced ourselves as children and how it affects the way we treat our children in turn.

Earlier I gave the example of a woman who had been brought up by parents who were very strict and constantly critical. We discussed how, as a result of what she experienced as a child, she will have the tendency to do one of two things. Either she will have internalized her parents attitudes (become strict and critical herself) and then inflict them on her children, or she will have flipped and gone the other way, deciding that her children will never be treated so harshly and instead become overly permissive with them. Either way, this woman's conditioning will cause her to feel very strongly that, whichever way she is treating them, it is correct. So which way is correct? The answer is neither. What is needed is a more objective view.

If you were to think of a line drawn down the exact center of a piece of paper, then list on that paper either of these ideas related to the 'correct' way of raising her children we would find them to be directly opposite of each other. One would be listed on the far left of that centerline, and the other on the far right. The objective is to get back to the center where we are neither too strict nor too permissive. This neutral place would be the most effective position for responding to her children's behavior and help them avoid the negative effects of either extreme.

The biggest problem for a parent wishing to move closer to the center in the treatment of their child will be their own conditioning. Take the mother who has become too permissive, when a situation occurs where her child indicates that they need something, she will tend to feel the very strong emotions she felt as a child when she needed something and was refused, *and she will feel too much.* Intellectually, she may understand this idea of getting back to center, but the emotions she feels will often be too powerful for her to refuse. In the end she is likely to give in to the child's request, not because it was necessarily reasonable, but because she needs to relive the emotions she was once again feeling, resulting from a similar, but not identical, childhood experience. From this, we can see that the parents behavior in this situation really has nothing to do with her child, but is entirely motivated by a need to deal with her own feelings tied to the past rather than what is actually happening in the present.

This conditioned reaction can be changed, but it will require that parents to begin observing themselves from their OO whenever they are dealing with their children. There is one way to know if you are acting objectively or from your conditioning. *Whenever you are reacting from your conditioning there will be an emotional charge that you feel,* such as the strong emotions the mother experienced in the situation just described. Probably, this feeling is something they have never been conscious of before, but with the help of your OO, you can begin to sense it and realize what it really is. It will become your guide to knowing if you are acting objectively, or simply reacting from a far less conscious place, your conditioning.

Typically, children become mirrors of their parents. Parents that are very angry around their children will find themselves faced eventually with very angry children or children who simply become withdrawn and may find other ways of dealing with those feelings, such as the use of alcohol or drugs. Watching your child from the perspective of your OO will begin to show you where their behavior is either left or right of that center place. Are they too often or too intensely angry? Too withdrawn? Do they often seem depressed? Do they appear to need to be constantly active? Do they lack adequate social skills? Do they lack self-confidence? Are they too aggressive? Are they overly competitive?

Once these imbalances are seen, your job will then be to help them get back to center, rather than just let them continue this extreme behavior for the rest of their life and severely limit any chance they might have for a happy marriage or to raise their children to be more emotionally stable. Remember, this can only be done from your OO with special attention paid to any emotions you feel in your reaction to their behavior.

If you have come to see that, at times, you were too angry with your child and now they too find themselves reacting with anger when it is not appropriate, or instead have simply shut down and repressed those feelings, you can help them get back to center. You would start this process by discussing what you have seen. There can't be any feelings of guilt on your part; you simply were not capable at the time of seeing what you were doing. *And there can't be any judgment toward your child.*

You start by discussing how you were brought up and how your anger resulted from your relationship with your parents, and your taking responsibility for having been to angry at times will open the door to truly effective communication. After you have done this and shown them how you treated them differently than you would have liked because of your conditioning, you can explain to them that your desire is for them to avoid the same mistake. Make sure you let them feel that you are acting from a place of love and compassion, *not anger and judgment.* Let them know you are in this together. You are going to work on your anger and invite them to do the same.

From this point on, when anger arises—yours or theirs—it will be seen differently by both of you. Instead of slipping into your conditioning and continuing to act from anger, you can move back to a more conscious place and reference your previous discussion. If you become angry and they point it out, thank them. And if they become angry, simply resume your previous loving and compassionate state and let them know you see it and want to help them move away from it.

Once you have started this process, you never again have to allow your anger to drive a wedge between the two of you and cause one or both of you to repeat dysfunctional behavior. Instead, your new approach will bring you closer together and improve your relationship dramatically.

If your child has come to respond to your anger by becoming withdrawn, the exact same process can be used and will bring you the same positive results. You will be teaching your child and incredible life lesson on how to effectively deal with their emotions in a way that will help them in every relationship they ever have, especially in their own marriage. You will have significantly increased their chances for having a happy, rather than dysfunctional, relationship. They will raise their own children with this same open communication, because they will have become able to 'see' rather than 'be' their conditioning. You will have truly given your child an incredible gift that will allow them to experience a level of intimacy and happiness they could never have had otherwise.

Always remember that the first step is seeing your own conditioning and how it has influenced your child. And letting them know what you have seen about yourself and how you take full responsibility for it and wish, with their help, to change it. This will make it much easier for them to model your behavior and begin taking responsibility for their own behavior. The change process will then be seen as something you are doing together. This is very different than what normally happens with the parent seeing the child as the problem, without seeing their part. Acting from that perspective will have exactly the opposite results you desire.

Also, if your child grows up in a home where the parents are working to solve their problems with each other in this same fashion, they will automatically pattern that behavior.

Two things will happen as a result of this process; your child will become emotionally more balanced and happy, and you yourself will be restored to a place of greater objectivity in dealing with them. Your own feelings will become more balanced and you will discover that you are becoming free of your own conditioning. The Audio Insights and podcasts available on our website www.dynamicnm.com offer more information for those who are interested.

Eighteen - Dealing with Family and Friends as We Become More Conscious.

"Too often we enjoy the comfort of opinion without the discomfort of thought" ~ John F. Kennedy

When you begin discussing the ideas in the book with others, it will help if you understand that anyone's vision of reality (yours or the person you are having a conversation with) will always be consistent with their level of understanding. That is, it will represent the truth—as they see it—at any given point in time and, according to their present level of development. However, until one has arrived at the Ultimate Truth, their vision will always be "relative." What they firmly believe to be true at one point along the way will change as their level of understanding (consciousness) increases.

A perfect example of this can be illustrated with the story of the three blind men who came upon an elephant. One touched its leg and believed it to be a tree. Another felt its side and thought it must be a wall. The third, who felt its snout, believed it was a snake. Then (as people dealing with partial or relative knowledge always have, and always will do) they argued with each other over who was correct. Never did they realize their differences could only be solved with the awareness of a greater and more inclusive truth i.e. that it was actually an elephant which could appear, from certain angles, to be something else. You may find yourself caught in this trap when attempting to share what you have learned with others.

Unfortunately, much of what you and others hear or read falls into this category of relative truth. Then of course, there is the other side of this problem to be considered. Even if everything written were the actual truth, rather than relative truth, it would still not be understood by many who read it. That is, it would be misunderstood, due to the inability of some readers, as a result of their level of consciousness, to comprehend what had been written. So what are we to do? How are we to separate actual truth from mere relative truth?

Fortunately, there is a way to quickly know which is which. All you need to do is apply what I refer to as the **Unity Test**. By simply asking yourself if what you are hearing *creates unity or creates separateness,* you will be able to determine *for yourself* the validity of what you hear. *This is an acid test you can apply to any religious or philosophical idea to judge its worth.*

For example, the statement *"Caucasians are superior to blacks,"* can easily be seen to create separateness, and is therefore, according to our test, false. Whereas the statement *"All people are equal."* creates unity, and can be seen to be correct. To come a little closer to home, the statement that *"Christianity is the only true religion."* again, can be seen as false. And the quote from Rumi *"Every prophet and every saint has a way, but all lead to God. All ways are really one."* can easily be seen as true. It is as simple as that. If you experiment with this, you will be surprised just how well it helps resolve conflicts of opinion.

There are certain kinds of questions, which do not lend themselves to the Unity Test, questions like "Was Christ greater than Buddha?" for instance. In these instances, it should be obvious that the question itself begs separateness, that is, any answer given to such a question would create separation and so of course, the Unity test cannot provide an answer as before. In cases like this, you simply apply the Unity test to the question itself and stop there.

Another problem you may encounter when attempting to share what you have seen from your increased level of consciousness can be someone's unwillingness to accept anything new. They may have a vested interest in holding on to a relative truth. For instance, if someone believes that, their group is in some way "special" or "better" than other's allows them to believe that they themselves, as a member of that group, are also special or better. There are those whose need to satisfy their ego or vanity is greater than their desire to know the truth. The information contained in this book, or your attempt to share it with another will not have any impact on such people.

Of course, the effects of egoism and vanity are not the only barriers to knowing the truth; any aspect of the conditioned-self can stand in the way, i.e. hate, pride, anger, lust, greed, etc. To a large extent, our level of understanding, the quality of our consciousness and our chances of seeing the truth are in direct proportion to our ability to rid ourselves of these impediments.

As one's level of awareness—consciousness—increases, they will see less and less dissimilarity, and realize more and more that there is but one immutable truth underlying all teachings related to raising your level of consciousness, and *eventually they will come to see that any view which does not express unity as false.* Before this point is reached however, it is all too easy to become confused by the apparent differences in the various instructions one encounters.

If you were to ask a man who had only seen one car in his life to describe it, he might say something like this: "A car is blue. It has the word Chevrolet attached to it. It has four doors and will help you get to your destination quickly."

Should you ask the same question of a man who has seen lots of cars his answer would be simpler, something like: "A car is something you can utilize to get to your destination more quickly." It is unlikely he would get caught up in arguments about the "true" color of a car or how many doors it "should" have. His view would be larger—much more objective. Alterations in a car's appearance would not prevent him from understanding its function. He would

204

see that a car is simply a vehicle to help you get to your destination faster and, that all the rest—the superficial differences—were unimportant.

When discussing philosophical questions you will see this same narrow view at times in others (such as the true color of a car being blue). Hopefully, you will begin to look past the superficial things, which tend to separate, and instead begin to see that one underlying immutable truth I mentioned earlier which unites all teachings. At least that is my wish.

In order for your understanding to grow, you must be willing to change your thinking, otherwise, it—and of course you—will remain the same. Just as those who once believed the world was flat had to change that to, the world "appears" flat but is actually round, so we must all allow a certain flexibility in our thinking if we are to see past appearances and continue learning. Our greatest enemy along our path toward becoming more conscious is our 'self' with its preconceived ideas and notions. **This book can give nothing to anyone that they are unwilling or unable to accept.**

As you begin to change, become more conscious, your behavior will change. You will begin to see certain negative interactions you previously engaged in with your friends and relatives in a new way and move away from them. Unless, those people around you are also doing the same type of inner work, they may see you as becoming a different person (which, of course, you are), but not necessarily for the better. They may have enjoyed the dramas, which you shared with them and will not be happy to let them go. They may even up the emotional intensity of certain situations in an attempt to draw you back into your former behavior.

This can be one of the most trying times on your journey to higher consciousness. You may find there are certain people you are very close to that are unable to accept the new you. This is where you will have to make a difficult choice...to continue to grow and risk the loss of a relationship you have considered very important, or remain in the same patterns of behavior as before to prevent this from happening. When this moment arrives—and it will, sooner or later—it will test your resolve to become more conscious like few other situations.

Nineteen - Expanding Your Consciousness Beyond Me, To We.

"A human being is part of a whole, called by us the Universe, a part limited in time and space. He experiences himself, his thoughts and feelings, as something separated from the rest, a kind of optical delusion of his consciousness. This delusion is a kind of prison for us, restricting us to our personal desires and to affection for a few persons nearest us. Our task must be to free ourselves from this prison by widening our circles of compassion to embrace all living creatures and the whole of nature in its beauty." ~ Albert Einstein

Thanks to the Quickening happening now and all of the people who are, and will be, working to become more conscious, our awareness will continue to expand to include not only ourselves, our relatives, or even our local city, but instead, *see and actually feel that the entire world and every being in it as part of a world community—a family—of which we are a member.* We will all become more and more conscious of what, at present, we've simply not cared to see, the true state of our community and the tremendous suffering occurring within it, for instance...

Quoting from the State of The Village Report:

If we could reduce the world's population to a village of precisely 100 people, with all existing human ratios remaining the same, the demographics would look something like this.

80 would live in substandard housing

67 would be unable to read

50 would be malnourished and 1 dying of starvation

33 would be without access to a safe water supply

39 would lack access to improved sanitation

24 would not have any electricity

7 People would have access to the Internet

1 would have a college education

33 would be receiving—and attempting to live on—only 3% of the income of our community.

Over 25,000 children die every day around the world. That is equivalent to 1 child dying every 3.5 seconds, 17-18 children dying every minute, and over 9 million dying each year.

We will gradually become less interested in ourselves specifically and more interested in the general welfare of others, regardless of their race, religion, gender, nationality, or location. This increasing awareness and the powerful feeling of compassion that results will lead us to begin to discover for ourselves the truth. Such as, if we woke up this morning with more health than sickness, we are luckier than **the million that will not survive this week.** If we are able to go to church, mosque or synagogue without fear of harassment, arrest, torture or death, we are happier, than 3 billion persons in this world. If there is a meal in our refrigerator, if we are dressed and have shoes, if we have a bed and a roof above our head, then we are better off than 75% of the people in this world. If we have a bank account and money in our pocket, we belong to 8% of well-provided people in this world. And finally, if we can read, we would be luckier than over 2 billion people in our community that can't. This knowledge will cause us to *feel* increasing compassion for all those far less fortunate than ourselves and compel us to take some action, however small, to do something to improve this situation.

We have a list of organizations on our web site www.dynamicnm.com who are attempting to help in a variety of ways and links to their web sites. If you wish to know more or, better yet, make some sort of contribution, please use these links to contact them today.

"Let us be the ones who say we do not accept that a child dies every three seconds simply because he does not have the drugs you and I have. Let us be the ones to say we are not satisfied that your place of birth determines your right to life. Let us be outraged, let us be loud, let us be bold." ~ Brad Pitt

Twenty - Our Community as a Source of Information and Support.

"What do we live for, if it is not to make life less difficult for each other?" ~ George Eliot

Thanks to the Quickening occurring now which is slowing bringing everyone to a place of higher consciousness, the possibility for change has never been greater. However, real change, that is, consciously reshaping your personality so that you might enjoy more happiness and success in your life—freeing yourself from your conditioning—is never easy. In fact, it can be at times extremely difficult. Once you have started this process, you will arrive at a point where you will begin to feel the exhilaration that comes from the freedom not to repeat that same old, tired, dysfunctional behavior. Once you get a taste of that freedom, you will want more, and still more. However, there will be those times when you hit major stumbling blocks and need help.

That is what our community is all about, people helping people become more conscious. You yourself may become involved in this process as you begin to discuss the ideas found in this book with others who are willing to hear. Your group can become a place where people begin helping each other to become more conscious, freer of their conditioning and the suffering it creates. Your behavior, as you move away from your own conditioning will have a positive effect on others you come in contact with even if you never discuss any of these ideas with them. Your greater consciousness and the new way you react to others will draw them up to a higher place. Just like negativity, consciousness is contagious.

The free podcasts, which are available on our web site www.dynamicnm.com can be a great source of inspiration as are the free monthly newsletters. There are many other resources on our site as well. You can e-mail us with questions and comments at any time, and we actually have a phone line for individuals or couples wanting to contact us directly.

One of the most effective things you can do is to create your own local community and support group by sharing the ideas in this book with others whom you believe are ready to hear them. Friends and relatives with whom you are able to talk, who are also doing this work, can be a wonderful resource. After joining our organization (which is completely free) we can help you contact others in your area involved in this work.

.

4037878

Made in the USA
Lexington, KY
15 December 2009